BONATTI'S
146 CONSIDERATIONS

Treatise 5 of Guido Bonatti's
Book of Astronomy

Translated by Benjamin N. Dykes, Ph.D.
From the 1491 and 1550 Latin Editions

The Cazimi Press
Minneapolis, Minnesota
2010

Published and printed in the United States of America
by the Cazimi Press
621 5th Avenue SE #25, Minneapolis, MN 55414

ISBN-13: 978-1-934586-07-5

PUBLISHER'S NOTE:

This reprint of Treatise 5 of Guido Bonatti's *Book of Astronomy* has been excerpted from the out-of-print 1st edition, published in 2007. The text reflects the original pagination, and has not been revised or updated to reflect new translation conventions or citations in more recent translations. The Tables of Figures and of Arabic Terms has been removed. A more recent version of Arabic terminology can be found at: www.bendykes.com/reviews/study.php.

For planetary configurations discussed in the 4th Consideration as well as much more horary material, students should consult my *Works of Sahl & Māshā'allāh* (2008) and *Bonatti on Horary* (2010), a reprint of Treatise 6 of the *Book of Astronomy*.

Dr. Benjamin N. Dykes
The Cazimi Press
April, 2010

TABLE OF CONTENTS

Book Abbreviations:

Abu 'Ali al-Khayyat:	*The Judgments of Nativities*	*JN*
Abū Ma'shar:	*Liber Introductorii Maioris ad Scientiam Iudiciorum Astrorum (Great Introduction to the Knowledge of the Judgments of the Stars)*	*Gr. Intr.*
	On Historical Astrology: the Book of Religions and Dynasties (On the Great Conjunctions)	*OGC*
	The Abbreviation of the Introduction to Astrology	*Abbr.*
	The Flowers of Abū Ma'shar	*Flowers*
Al-Biruni:	*The Book of Instruction in the Elements of the Art of Astrology*	*Instr.*
Māshā'allāh:	*On Reception*	*OR*
	On the Revolutions of the Years of the World	*De Rev. Ann.*
Pseudo-Ptolemy:	*Centiloquium (Centiloquy)*	*Cent.*
Ptolemy	*Tetrabiblos*	*Tet.*
Sahl ibn Bishr:	*On Elections*	*On Elect.*
	On Questions	*On Quest.*
	Introduction	*Introduct.*
'Umar al-Tabarī:	*Three Books of Nativities*	*TBN*
Vettius Valens:	*The Anthology*	*Anth.*

TREATISE 5:
146 CONSIDERATIONS

On the Considerations which concern judgments,
according to the motions and things signified
by the stars, and on certain headings pertaining
to the introduction of judgments

And there are 146 chapters or Considerations in it

However,[1] of those things which pertain to judgments, there are six that are to be considered from the beginning, as will be discussed below in its own place: first, nations[2] and the generation of nations; second, the constitution of households, and families, [and] the arranging[3] of individual households; third, the disposing of the dealings of wealthy and powerful people; fourth, the considerations of individuals of the human race; fifth, elections or the beginnings of actions; sixth, both universal and particular questions—and thus astronomical judgments can be reached. But before they may be reached there are certain things to be set out in advance, which seem to have to do with the subject of them, such as considering the manner of inquiring into it [for] someone who intends to ask about some matter, and even to observe other considerations, and other ways which it is necessary for you to consider in the business of judgments.

And there are 146 Considerations, which it would be impossible to apply all of them at one and the same time. But after I have named them all to you, I will tell you in the end those without which an astrologer cannot judge perfectly.[4] But nevertheless, first I will tell you the way which anyone [who] wished to ask something from an astrologer must observe: because to judge about things that

---

[1] When translating this Treatise, it became abundantly clear that Coley's translation (also known as the *Anima Astrologiae*) was more a paraphrase. Not only did he not translate the *146 Considerations* literally, but he sometimes simply omitted passages and sentences altogether.
[2] *Nationes.* Bonatti means this in the terms of ethnic groups or clans.
[3] *Ordinationes.* Or perhaps, "ranking."
[4] This probably refers to the 143rd Consideration.

are to be,[5] as it is sometimes called, is a most difficult thing, nor can can it be judged about things that are to be definitely [and] to a fine point; however it can be judged near to the truth, to which it is likened enough, and truly approaches. Nor does it differ from it by much–almost imperceptibly. And even though it is a most difficult thing to judge[6] about things that are to be, nor however is it a labor to be avoided, for indeed we strive to know everything concerning judgments that can ever be attained by the human mind. And because inferior things are ruled by superior things, as all unanimously agree (and it is true, as is said elsewhere), and the disposition of the superior bodies can be known by the dimensions of their motions, which have been discovered exactly by experienced people, and publicly proven, we can judge about things that are to be, and which of those motions falls together [with it], and to predict what is to come.

For this Art has precepts; for the precepts of astronomy are its end; and its end (as is touched on elsewhere) is the judgments that it makes regardless of what those who strive to reprove astronomy say (who seem to want to say it is nothing). For something is not an Art if it does not have its own precepts. [But] it *is* an Art (as was said elsewhere), which no one denies. Therefore it has an end, and its end is judgment. And the astrologer must consider judgments, and judgments are about accidents which are impressed in inferior things from the motions of the superior bodies, and from their qualities on account of their effects in them.

THE 1ST CONSIDERATION, on those things which move a man to pose a question (and there are three motions).[7] The first is the motion of the soul,[8] when someone is moved by his intention to pose a question. The second is the motion of the superior bodies, namely when someone asks what they are impressing into the quaesited thing, what will come of it. The third is the motion of the free will, which can itself be an act of the one asking. Because even though the soul is moved to ask, it does not suffice unless the superior bodies lead him to pose the question; nor does the motion of the stars suffice, unless from the motion of the free will the act of asking is reached.

---

[5] *Iudicare de futuris.* An alternate way of putting this is, "to judge about future things." But I have tried to preserve the sense of the future participle.

[6] Reading *iudicare* for *iudicari.*

[7] *Motus.* There is a close relation between a motion and a motive, since a motive is what moves one to action. Here and throughout Tr. 6, Bonatti will use this term to speak about people who are moved to ask questions.

[8] *Animae.*

THE 2ND CONSIDERATION is on the way which anyone must observe, who wants to ask something of an astrologer. And it is when he himself wishes to ask the astrologer about present things, or past things, or future things: he must observe this manner of asking, plainly that he ought to pray to the Lord God, from Whom every good beginning leads, and to entreat Him (with all devotion and with a contrite spirit) that it should fall to him to reach to an understanding of the truth of those things about which he intends to ask. Then with this truth[9] he ought to go to the astrologer with intention concerning that about which he is going to ask, and about which he proposed to ask, and the intention for which he retains in his heart for a day and a night (or more), not touched by just any motion of the mind (as sometimes many impertinent people are wont to do, as is said elsewhere). And thus He who spoke, who gave so you may seek, will add [to it] so that you may find.[10]

I estimate [that] it ought to happen this way in any question, unless perhaps there is at some time a sudden reason, emerging suddenly, which demands a sudden question and a sudden response which does not admit of delay (as often happens); the beginning [statement][11] of which, however, is always the name of the Highest; for certain people sometimes do otherwise, and for that reason they come to be deceived in themselves, and they sometimes pressure the astrologer—or rather, they often lie; for a stupid querent makes the responding wise man deviate sometimes; and men, not knowing the folly of him who asks poorly, sometimes defame and revile [the astrologer] when the astrologer is not guilty [of deserving to be] defamed or reviled.[12]

THE 3RD CONSIDERATION is to see in how many ways the planets may operate in inferior things on account of the diversity of the qualities of the aforesaid motions. And there are 16 ways by which occur the diversities of operating, and the effecting of all things which come to be and are perfected; and of those which do not come to be, and are not perfected; and of those which partly

---

[9] Reading *veritate* for *veritatis*.

[10] *Et sic qui dixit qui dedit ut quaeras, addet ut invenias.* This is Bonatti's astrological version of Matthew 7:7: "Ask, and it shall be given you; seek, and ye shall find; knock, and it shall be opened unto you." *Quaero* means both to seek and to ask, and is the verb used both in the Vulgate and in referring to horary questions.

[11] *Exordium.* This term means both the beginning of a rhetorical speech, although it also refers to the beginning of rituals, and Bonatti seems to invoke the latter sense when he speaks of the importance of calling upon God's aid. Bonatti must be conscious of his word choice since he almost always speaks of a beginning (*initio, principium*) in terms of the beginnings of actions.

[12] This paragraph was ignored in Coley's version.

come to be and are perfected; and partly do not come to be nor are perfected, which are discussed below.[13]

THE 4TH CONSIDERATION is of the causes of things helping matters so they come to be, and are perfected, and those which prohibit matters so they do not come to be, nor are they perfected; and what are the causes destroying matters after they were perfected (which often happens). And they come to be in 16 ways, as I said, according to 16 diverse motions, *etc.*[14]

Of which the first is, the arrival or advancement of things, or in things, which the philosophers call *al-iqbāl.*[15]

The second is deterioration [or worsening], which they call *al-idbār.*[16]

The third is conjunction, or turning back, which they call *al-'ittisal.*[17]

The fourth is separation, or disjoining, which they call *al-'insirāf.*[18]

The fifth is the transfer of light, which they call *an-naql.*[19]

The sixth is collection or aggregation, which they call *al-jam'.*[20]

---

[13] See the 4th Consideration, immediately following.

[14] In what follows I have replaced Bonatti's badly Latinized Arabic with the correct Arabic transliterations, in order to preserve the continuity between the Latin authors and the Arabic texts from which they inherited the astrological tradition. Some of these terms come through comparison with the Arabic editions of Abū Ma'shar's *Abbreviation* and al-Qabīsī's *Introduction* and Sahl's *Introduction* (see Bibliography). I am indebted to Terry Linder for helping me with the Arabic, and in seeing where Bonatti (or his typesetters) attributed the Arabic to the incorrect Latin terms.

[15] Lat. *Alocohol,* from *al-wusūl* (الوصول), "arrival, reaching destination," with the Latin pronounced with a soft *c*. But Abū Ma'shar (*Abbr.* III.4), al-Qabīsī (I.71) and Sahl use *al-iqbāl* (الاقبال, Lat. *icbel*), "advance," so I adopt it here. A planet is in "advance" if it is angular or succeedent.

[16] Lat. *Aliber,* from Ar. الادبار, "retreat" (Abū Ma'shar, *Abbr.* III.5; al-Qabīsī I.71). Bonatti's text here is based on Sahl, whose Latin text uses "deterioration" (*deterioratio*). But this is not supported by Abū Ma'shar or al-Qabīsī, and is probably a result of a conflation in the lists. A planet is in retreat if it is cadent.

[17] Lat. *Alitisal* (sometimes *Alitifal*), Ar. الإتصال, "application" (Abū Ma'shar, *Abbr.* III.13; al-Qabīsī, III.11). The reference to "turning back" seems to be a mistake, since that refers to *al-idbār*, which Bonatti calls "worsening."

[18] Lat. *Alinchirat,* Ar. الإنصراف (Abū Ma'shar, *Abbr.* III.14; al-Qabīsī, III.11).

[19] Lat. *Annecad,* Ar. النَقْل, "the transfer/relaying" (Abū Ma'shar, *Abbr.* III.23; al-Qabīsī, III.14).

[20] Lat. *Algemei,* Ar. الجَمْع, "the gathering/bringing together" (Abū Ma'shar, *Abbr.* III.25).

The seventh is forbidding or prohibition, which they call *al-man'*.[21]

The eighth is called reception, which they call *al-qubūl*.[22]

The ninth is voiding of course, which they call *khāl as-sayr*.[23]

The tenth is granting or permission, which they call *ghafra l-qubūl*.[24]

The eleventh is the return of virtue or disposition, which they call *ar-radd*.[25]

The twelfth is the pushing of virtue, which they call *daf' al-quwwah*.[26]

The thirteenth is the pushing of disposition, which they call *daf' t-adbīr*.[27]

The fourteenth is virtue or strength, which they call *al-qawwīah*.[28]

The fifteenth is weakness, which they call *ad-d'af*.[29]

---

[21] Lat. *Almana*, Ar. المَنْع, "the prevention/interdiction" (Abū Ma'shar, *Abbr.* III.28; al-Qabīsī, III.16).

[22] Lat. *Alcobol*, Ar. القُبُول, "the reception/admission," (Abū Ma'shar, *Abbr.* III. 52; al-Qabīsī, III.19).

[23] Lat. *Galaalocir*, Ar. خال السير, "void of course" (Abū Ma'shar, *Abbr.* III.21; al-Qabīsī, III.12). Both the 1550 and 1491 editions mistakenly assign this word to the tenth motion ("granting or permission").

[24] "The pardoning of the admission," (غفر القبول), Lat. *Gafralcobol*. In the 1550 edition this is mistakenly assigned to the ninth motion ("voiding of course"). This is listed in Sahl as "reception" (*receptio*), but I do not find it as an independent concept in either Abū Ma'shar's or al-Qabīsī's lists.

[25] Lat. *Alteat*. This must be Abū Ma'shar's, Sahl's, and al-Qabīsī's "returning," الرد (Abū Ma'shar, *Abbr.* III.35; al-Qabīsī, III.20).

[26] Lat. *Dalpha alchoa*, Ar. دفع القوة, "The pushing of strength/power (Abū Ma'shar, *Abbr.* III.31; al-Qabīsī, III.18).

[27] Lat. *Dafaaredbit*, Ar. دفع التدبير, "The pushing of management," also known as "pushing counsel" (Abū Ma'shar, *Abbr.* III.34).

[28] Lat. *Alcoevah*, Ar. القوية, "strength." This member of the list comes from Sahl (Lat. *alcdetib*), who seems to use it as a general consideration of various types of strength.

[29] "Weakness," (الضعف), Lat. *Adirof*.

The sixteenth is the condition of the Moon, which they call *khamalu l-qamar*,[30] which is an evil condition and the corruption of the Moon, just as the ancient sages said.

THE 5TH CONSIDERATION is in how many ways such a condition of the Moon occurs.[31] And the philosophers said that this happens in 10 ways.[32] But it seems to me that 7 could be added, and thus there will be 17 ways by which impediments and detriments come to be in all matters which are impeded–and in all beginnings, and in all questions, and in all journeys, and in all nativities, and in all things which we want to do or intend to do.

Of which the first is when the Moon is combust, namely within the rays of the Sun, before him by less than 15° (namely from behind the Sun, when she goes toward him);[33] and after him by less than 12° (that is, when she goes away from him, so that she goes out from under his rays).[34] Because it is possible that she may appear from under his rays.[35] And it is a greater impediment for her when she goes toward the Sun, than it is when she goes away from him: because when she goes away, and is separated from him by 5°, she is said to have escaped, even though she is not wholly liberated–just like when a fever leaves a sick person, because even though he is weak and broken, still he is said to be liberated, because he is already untroubled about the strength that is going to come.

The second is when she is in the degrees of her own descension, namely in the third degree of Scorpio (or in the whole of Scorpio), and in all of Capricorn; or [when] she is joined to a planet in its own descension, namely that the planet is in its own descension or the descension of the Moon–as when she is joined to the Sun, and he is in Scorpio or in Capricorn; or the Sun is in its own descension, namely in Aquarius or in Libra (i.e., in its nineteenth degree or in the whole of Libra); or if she were

---

[30] "The weakness/obscurity of the Moon," (خمل القمر), Lat. *Gnaymel alchamaur*.
[31] I.e., the last of the above modes/motions in the 4th Consideration.
[32] The following list is based on either Sahl (*Introduct.*) or al-Rijāl (p. 303).
[33] That is, when she is in an earlier zodiacal degree.
[34] I.e., in later zodiacal degrees than the Sun's.
[35] Bonatti is probably saying that we maintain these orbs *despite* the fact that the Moon may be visible in fewer than that many degrees from the Sun (although whether this is true or not, I do not know).

joined to Mars, and he were in Libra or in Taurus, or in the twenty-eighth degree of Cancer (or in the whole of Cancer). And understand this about all of the other planets.[36]

The third is when she is in the combust degrees, of which the worse ones are the 12° which are before the degree that is directly opposite the degree in which the Sun is (in whatever degree the Sun was).

The fourth is when she is joined to one of the malefics [by corporal conjunction], or in its opposition or square aspect without perfect reception, like if she were joined to Saturn or Mars; less bad, though, would be if perfect reception were to intervene, because then they impede less. In all of the other places they impede her from the aforesaid aspects, and from the corporal conjunction, unless she were in places in which the malefic had two of the lesser dignities—like Saturn in the last 4° of Aries, in which he has his bound and triplicity; and in the last 4° of Gemini, in which he likewise has two dignities; and like Mars in the last 10° of Pisces, in which he has [his] face and triplicity.[37] And understand this about all the other signs and places in which they have two of the lesser dignities.

The fifth is when she is with the Head of the Dragon or its Tail, so that there are less than 12° between them, because that is the boundary within which the Moon is eclipsed.

The sixth is when she is in Gemini, which is the twelfth sign from her own domicile.[38]

The seventh is when she is in the ends of the signs, which are the bounds of the malefics, except for the last 6° of Leo,[39] which are the bound of

---

[36] This Consideration presents two lessons about Bonatti's astrology. First, he does not clearly distinguish between what we would call the weakness of "detriment" and "fall," calling them both a "descension" (*descensio*). Likewise in Tr. 6, he sometimes uses *descensio* and *casus* ("fall") interchangeably. Second, while he gives a nod to the traditional view that a planet's fall is in a specific degree of the sign opposite that of its exaltation, he plainly wants to treat the whole sign itself as the sign of fall.

[37] This description follows Ptolemy's bounds (*Tet.* I.21), since the Egyptian bounds allot the last 5° of Aries to Saturn, not 4°.

[38] Bonatti is clearly referring to whole-sign houses here.

[39] In Ptolemy's own bounds, this should read 5°.

Jupiter.[40] But in its first 6° she is impeded, because they are the bound of Saturn. But you could perhaps say that she is impeded in the first 6° of Cancer, which are the bound of Mars–however, she is not impeded there like in the other bounds of the malefics, since something is removed from it: because Cancer is her domicile, and her greatest strength.

The eighth is when she is in the sixth, eighth, ninth, or twelfth from the Ascendant, [and] not received, or joined to a planet in one of them; or [if] she is in the third, since the third [sign] is among those cadent from the angles (but because she is said to rejoice in it, she is not impeded in it as she is in the others that are cadent from the angles).

The ninth is when she is from the fifteenth degree of Libra up to the end of the fifteenth degree of Scorpio, the which 30° are the *via combusta*.[41]

The tenth is when she is void in course, namely joined to none of the planets by body or by aspect; or she is uncivilized or feral, which happens when she is void in course and is in a place in which she has no dignity.

The eleventh is when she is slow in course, because then she is likened to a retrograde planet.

The twelfth is when she is in a failure of her light, so that nothing or very little of her can be seen [while] going to combustion, which happens at the end of the lunar month.

The thirteenth is when she is besieged between two malefics impeding her.

The fourteenth is when she is in the azemene degrees.

The fifteenth is when she is in the welled degrees.

---

[40] This is according to the traditional *mis*understanding of Ptolemy's bounds. Ptolemy's own system gives the last 5° of Leo to Mars.

[41] The "combust way." These degrees (corresponding to the pans of Libra) are also the claws of the constellation of Scorpio. One wonders whether the *via combusta* should be linked to these fixed stars, and not anymore to the tropical signs of Scorpio and Libra.

The sixteenth is when she is in the smoky degrees.

The seventeenth is when she is in the dark degrees, concerning all of which you have tables noted above, in the first Treatise of this work.[42]

THE 6TH CONSIDERATION is another mode of the weakness of the planets (not departing much from the aforesaid), which comes about in 10 ways:

Of which the first is when a planet is cadent from the angles and from the Ascendant (so that it does not aspect it).[43]

The second is when a planet is retrograde.

The third is when it is combust, that is, [for a superior planet] by 15° in front of the Sun, and less so[44] after him: indeed the inferiors are impeded more when they are after the Sun, and less so when they are in front of him (when they are direct; to the contrary when retrograde).[45]

The fourth is when one of them is in the opposition or the corporal conjunction or the square aspect of one of the malefics (or more of them) without reception.

The fifth is when it is besieged [or occupied] by the two malefics, namely so that it is separated from one, and is joined to the other without perfect reception by domicile or exaltation, or by two of the lesser dignities (which are bound, triplicity, and face).

The sixth is when a planet is joined to a planet in its own descension, or in its own fall, namely in opposition to its own domicile or exaltation.

---

[42] Actually they are in Tr. 2, suggesting perhaps this Treatise was written earlier.

[43] In later Treatises Bonatti makes clear that orbs do not matter here–it is to be understood either as whole signs or quadrant houses (which he does not always clearly distinguish in this context). Being "cadent from the angles" means being in the 12th, 9th, 6th, and 3rd; being "cadent from the Ascendant" means being in the 12th, 8th, 6th, and 2nd (since these signs or houses do not have a classical aspect to the 1st house.

[44] "Less so" here means "less afflicted," not "fewer degrees." Recall that in the case of the Moon, she was no longer combust after 12°. Bonatti does not always distinguish being under the sunbeams and being combust.

[45] By "in front of," Bonatti means "in a later zodiacal degree"; by "after," he means "in an earlier zodiacal degree."

The seventh, when it is joined to a planet cadent from the Ascendant, or it is separated from a planet who was receiving it and is joined to another who does not receive it.

The eighth is when it is peregrine, that is, when it is in a place in which it does not have any dignity; or they are superiors followed by the Sun, or the inferiors pursue him.[46]

The ninth is when a planet is with the Head of the Dragon or its Tail, without latitude.

The tenth is when it is a planet impeding itself, that is, when it is in the seventh from its own domicile (namely, feral)[47] or not received.

These are the ten impediments of the planets, by which impediments come to be in nativities, in questions, journeys, and in all works which we intend to do or begin. You must know all of these kinds of impediments of the planets. And there are other ways which you must know, certain ones of which I will make mention to you, which seem to be more necessary for you to know. Because it would be difficult, or rather most difficult, to consider all of those ways; for as I said it would be impossible for you to apply them all at one and the same time. But I will tell you those which are more necessary for you, and without which you could not judge perfectly. I will perhaps name others for you, but will not expound all of them lest it generate weariness in you; of which certain ones are most strongly good, certain ones more strongly good, certain ones strongly good, certain ones weakly good, certain ones more weakly good, certain ones most weakly good, certain ones hidden, certain ones manifest, certain ones are most strongly evil, certain ones more strongly evil, certain ones strongly evil,

---

[46] *Vel sint superiores secuti a Sole, vel inferiores insequantur eum.* Coley's translation is somewhat ambiguous because of his use of "follow" for both the superiors and inferiors. Bonatti is saying that the superiors are in a worse condition when they are in later degrees than the Sun and he is approaching them from behind (due to his faster motion), and likewise for the inferiors when they are "pursuing" him, which must mean that *he* is in a later degree and they are approaching *him* from behind (on account of *their* faster motion). It is not so much a question of rising after or before the Sun, but rather of coming close to his beams.

[47] This definition of ferality or "wildness" seems to be an extension of the usual sense: if a planet is in its detriment then it is as though it has been thrown out of its home and so is in the "wilderness."

certain ones weakly evil, certain ones more weakly evil, certain ones most weakly evil.

THE 7TH CONSIDERATION is that you beware of those ways by which an astrologer can err, of which the wise[48] named four.

The first is if the querent did not know how to ask.

The second, if the astrologer were to take the shadow in an uneven place, or with a false instrument.

The third, if he did not know whether the Sun had already receded from the line of the Midheaven or whether it was on the line, or ahead of it, or after it.[49]

The fourth, if the benefics and the malefics were equal, whence you ought not to receive the question then, if you can avoid it.

But to me it seems that three other ways could be added, by which the astrologer can err:

One, namely if the querent were to come to him in order to test him, as some people sometimes do, who say "Let's go to such-and-such astrologer, and let's ask him about such-and-such a matter, and we'll see if he has told us the truth"–just as the Jews did to the Lord Jesus Christ.

Likewise it seems that the astrologer can err by another way, namely if the querent does not ask from an intention, just as certain people sometimes do when they meet an astrologer, or when they go on behalf of the affairs of others: they think about some matter about which *they* wish to ask the astrologer, and thus they unexpectedly ask, and then error can come into play there.[50] And you could say, "how will I be able to know whether the querent asks from an intention or not, or he asks for reasons of testing, or

---

[48] These first four ways are attributed to Māshā'allāh in the *On Interpretations*.

[49] I believe that by "ahead of," Bonatti means "in an earlier degree than the cusp's"; by "after," he means "in a later degree than the cusp's." See my Introduction.

[50] Emphasis mine. In other words, instead of restricting their trip to the astrologer to the concerns of the true querent, they cause confusion by asking for themselves. See my comments on "roots" in the Introduction, Section E.

not?" To which I say to you that it seems to me a very hard and difficult thing; but I have been tested many times, and I have found [the following] to be true, because I took the hour of the question, and I looked at its Ascendant, and if I found in the eastern line that the Ascendant of some sign was between the end of one sign and the beginning of the next,[51] I said that he was not asking from an intention; or that he was asking for reasons of testing; and I found many who confided to me that it was so, and they reckoned afterwards that I knew something else which they had believed before; and they were brought to faith in the Art when beforehand they had had none. And when I found [such an] Ascendant for someone, as I stated, I used to say to him, "Brother, do not exhaust me unless you are asking from an intention, because I suspect that you want to deceive me by not proposing this question like you were supposed to. But if you want me to work on your affairs, recompense me for my labor"–and immediately, if it was a deception, he went away.

The astrologer can err by another, third way, namely if the Lord of the Ascendant and the Lord of the hour were not the same, or the Lord of the Ascendant and the Lord of the hour were not of the same triplicity, or were not of the same complexion as the Ascendant. For if you were to find it so, the question will not be rooted,[52] just as I have experienced many times.

Therefore I have recited this to you, so that you may know what men you ought to look for. Because, as the philosopher said,[53] the matter proceeds according to the quality of the querent's concern, and according to how he came to you by necessity, as though sad, or meditating, and thus hoping that you could know how to respond to him [and] to his question; for you are able to look for him with confidence.

THE 8TH CONSIDERATION is that you see and consider how many of the aforesaid ways, or the aforesaid considerations (which you must use in judg-

---

[51] This could be the origin of the famous consideration in Lilly (*Christian Astrology* I, p. 122), that horary questions are either invalid or not worth asking (or already decided) if the degree of the Ascendant is within 3° of the beginning or end of the rising sign. But note that Bonatti does not actually say what the span of degrees should be.

[52] *Radicalis*. See Introduction.

[53] Bonatti's "philosopher" is probably Māshā'allāh or Sahl.

ments) you ought to consider, which are thirty-one: namely the 17[54] aforesaid ones on the impediments of the Moon and the 10 by which the planets are impeded and weakened; and the 4 by which the planets rejoice, as I told you above in the chapter on the joys of the planets.

Of which, of the four lesser ones, the first is to look at the place in which any planet rejoices, like Mercury who rejoices in the Ascendant, the Moon in the 3rd, Venus in the 5th, Mars in the 6th, the Sun in the 9th, Jupiter in the 11th, Saturn in the 12th.

The second is when a planet is in its own domicile in which it rejoices (as was said elsewhere), like Saturn who rejoices in Aquarius, Jupiter in Sagittarius, Mars in Scorpio, the Sun in Leo, Venus in Taurus, Mercury in Virgo, the Moon in Cancer. And do not let it annoy you if sometimes I will reiterate something to you of those things which were said elsewhere, because it is easier for you to see what you want where and when it is necessary, [than] to look elsewhere.[55]

The third is when the diurnal planets (who are Saturn, Jupiter, the Sun, and Mercury) are with diurnal ones in the east, and they are oriental from the Sun, and they are next to the oriental line; and the nocturnal ones (who are Mars, Venus, the Moon and Mercury) are with nocturnal ones in the west, and occidental from the Sun, and especially next to the western line.[56]

The fourth is when the three superiors (namely Saturn, Jupiter, Mars) are in masculine quarters (which are from the cusp of the 10th house up to the cusp of the 1st house, and from the cusp of the 4th house up to the cusp of the 7th house); and when Venus and the Moon are in feminine quarters (which are from the cusp of the Ascendant up to the cusp of the 4th, and from the cusp of the 7th house up to the cusp of the 10th house).

---

[54] The text reads: 30…16, apparently miscounting the list of 17 impediments of the Moon. I have corrected the numbers to read 31…17.

[55] Bonatti will make good on this promise–and complain about it–many times in Tr. 6.

[56] This point seems to be a combination of *halb* (see Introduction) and Ptolemy's doctrine of eastern and western quarters.

Indeed Mercury rejoices with masculine planets in masculine quarters, and with the feminine planets in feminine quarters.[57]

THE 9TH CONSIDERATION is to look at the ways helping or harming in matters so that they come to be or do not come to be—both the open [helpers and harmers] and the hidden ones, the good ones and the bad ones. For there are 21:

Of which the first is the strongest hidden helper.
The second is a stronger hidden helper.
The third is a strong hidden helper.
The fourth is a weak hidden helper.
The fifth is a weaker hidden helper.
The sixth is the weakest hidden helper.
The seventh is the strongest open helper.
The eighth is a stronger open helper.
The ninth is a strong open helper.
The tenth is a weak open helper.
The eleventh is a weaker open helper.
The twelfth is the weakest open helper.
The thirteenth is the strongest hidden harmer.
The fourteenth is a stronger hidden harmer.
The fifteenth is a strong hidden harmer.
The sixteenth is a weak hidden harmer.
The seventeenth is a weaker hidden harmer.
The eighteenth is the weakest hidden harmer.
The nineteenth is the strongest open harmer.
The twentieth is a stronger open harmer.
The twenty-first is a strong open harmer.

Of all of which I will make mention to you. And this is a hidden and secret matter among the secrets of the judgments of the stars, about which the ancients were not concerned; and they said nothing openly about it which I found, except that 'Ali seemed to have touched on it somewhat in his exposi-

---

[57] It is not clear from this sentence whether Mercury need only be in the given quarter to rejoice with (or be counted with) them; or whether they must be in a quarter appropriate to them *and* in aspect to Mercury, or what.

tion of the 29th saying of the *Centiloquy* of Ptolemy.[58] Nor do I believe they dismissed them on account of ignorance, but more likely because they were not accustomed to it, and because they did not want to cause weariness in their listeners or readers, nor to burden their minds. For they judged according to how they found the planets disposed in the houses [and] in the signs, and according to their strength and their weakness, and likewise according to the Part of Fortune, and according to certain other things which it seemed to them to be among them. But in your judgments you ought to consider those things which they considered in theirs, and besides that whatever other connected thing[59] you can consider.

For when you erect some figure you ought to consider and see the ruler[60] of the quaesited matter, or thing undertaken, or a thing to be begun or to be done, [to see] if one of the fixed stars which is of its nature is in a place in which he has domicile or exaltation, and is with him in the same minute: because then the star will help the significator in such a way, and to such an extent that the matter will be perfected, even beyond the intention of the querent or the one beginning it or doing it. And this is the strongest hidden helper. For he will not know whence it will happen to him. If indeed the star were with the significator in the same degree, from one minute to 16' in front, or up to 5' behind,[61] it will help him, but not very much. And this is a stronger secret helper. If indeed it were with him in the same degree from 16' up to in the fiftieth,[62] it will help less again; and this is a strong hidden helper. If indeed it were with him in the same degree, in a place in which the significator had two of the lesser dignities, in the same minute or from 1' up to in the sixteenth,[63] it will help him less again. And this will be a weak hidden helper. If indeed it were in the same degree, distant from the significator by more than 16' up to in the fiftieth,[64] it will help him less than that, and this will be a weaker hidden helper. If indeed it were in a place in which the significator did not have any dignity, it will help him somewhat, but practically imperceptibly. And this will be the weakest hidden helper.

---

[58] Bonatti is perhaps referring to 'Ali ibn Ridwān. The text reads "23rd", but Bonatti must be referring to Aph. 29 (which pertains to fixed stars), so I have corrected the text here.

[59] *De contingentibus.*

[60] *Dominatorem.* This is undoubtedly either the Lord or the *al-mubtazz* of the matter.

[61] I believe by "in front," Bonatti means "in a later degree than the significator's"; by "behind," he means "in an earlier degree than the significator's."

[62] *Usque in 50.* This is another example of the ambiguous use of Arabic numerals to denote both cardinal and ordinal numbers in Bonatti.

[63] *Usque in 16.*

[64] *Usque in 50.*

And the harmers are contrary to the helpers. For if the planet who was the significator of some matter were in such a place in which he did not have any dignity, with one of the fixed stars which was contrary to his nature in the same minute, it will harm him, and will not permit the matter to be perfected, and it will seem, by the figure erected for the matter, that the matter ought to be perfected, and then the astrologer will be responsible, and will be unjustly held in slight esteem, and for a reason he did not merit; and astronomy will be said by idiots and those blaspheming it, to be erroneous, and to be nothing. And this will be the strongest hidden harmer. If indeed [the significator] were with [the star] in a place in which it had one of the aforesaid lesser dignities, outside of the first minute up to the sixteenth,[65] then it will harm less and will impede less. And this will be the stronger hidden harmer. But if it were in a place in which it had two of the lesser dignities, in the same degree with one of the stars themselves, from beyond 16', it will then harm less again. And this will be a strong hidden harmer. If indeed the star were in the domicile or the exaltation of the significator, not in the same minute, but in another outside it, up to 16',[66] it will harm less than that. And this will be a weak hidden harmer. If however the star were with the significator in [its] domicile or exaltation from 16' up to the fiftieth, it will harm less again. And this will be the weaker hidden harmer. If for instance the star were with the significator in the same degree, in one of the greater dignities from 50' up the end of the degree, it will harm less again. And this will be the weakest hidden helper.

However, the fixed stars, which are of the natures of the planets and of their contraries, will not be named here (for it would be a lengthy statement); but in the Treatise on revolutions I will tell you certain ones which it will be necessary for you to consider in any revolution; I will tell you certain ones in the Treatise on nativities, certain others in the Treatise on rains–if the goodness of God will provide me life, with the integrity of body, to finish this work.

On the aforesaid modes, which are the strongest good ones, etc.,
and which are the strongest bad ones

But I do not want to forget before I tell you the ways (about which I made mention above), namely which are the strongest good ones, *etc.*, and which are the strongest bad ones, *etc.*; and they all are open and not hidden, whether they are good or bad.

---

[65] *Usque in 16.*
[66] *Usque in 16. minuta.*

The strongest open good one is when a planetary significator of some matter is in its own domicile, in an angle, in the very minute of the cusp, direct, fast in course, received, free from any impediment–which happens most rarely. The stronger open good one is when the significator is in an angle, in its own domicile or exaltation, by 1° ahead of the line or by 2° after,[67] free from the malefics, and received, which more rarely happens. The strong open good one is when the significator is in an angle, in its own domicile or exaltation, ahead of the line by 3° or 5° after it.

The weak open good one is when the planet is in two of its own lesser dignities, in an angle by 5° ahead or 15° after,[68] or if it is in its own domicile or exaltation, in a succeedent to an angle, free from the malefics. A weaker open good one is when the planetary significator is in its own domicile or in its exaltation, or in two of its other lesser dignities, in the cadents, aspecting the Ascendant. The weakest open good one is when the planetary significator is in one of its greater dignities, or in two of its lesser ones, not aspecting the Ascendant, or in only one of its lesser dignities, aspecting it, or joined to a planet aspecting the Ascendant and having testimony in it.

The strongest open bad one is when the significator is in a place in which he has no dignity, no joy, not received, besieged by the two malefics, cadent from an angle, and cadent from the Ascendant, and even more so if it were joined with one of the malefic fixed stars.

And there are other ways besides the aforesaid, [some] helping and others harming, both hidden and open, and they come to be through the conjunctions and aspects of the planets, all of which it would take a long time to list individually here, [and] about which I am not making mention (but it will happen with certain ones of them in this Treatise), for the account would be prolonged, [and] would bring about irritation to the listener and reader. Nor even am I giving examples of all of the aforesaid to you, because of the

---

67 I believe that by "ahead of," Bonatti means "in an earlier degree than the cusp's"; by "after," he means "in a later degree than the cusp's." See my Introduction.
68 I believe that by "ahead of," Bonatti means "in an earlier degree than the cusp's"; by "after," he means "in a later degree than the cusp's." See my Introduction.

excessive prolixity of words. But I will tell you in the end about the considerations or chapters which principally pertain to a first glance at judgments.[69]

OF WHICH THE FIRST IS THE 9TH CONSIDERATION, and it is that you know that the Moon (above all other planets) has a similarity with inferior, generated things, namely to the kinds[70] of *genera* and the individuals of kinds;[71] and this happens to her because of her own effects which she has in all terrestrial things and from the frequent revolutions–the which revolutions she makes about the elements, and around things made from elements,[72] which is because of her close approach to the earth.

She even has a smaller circle than [any] other of the planets. For within her circle is not contained any other circle, but only the elements and the other corruptible things. For indeed, the Moon is the mediator between the stars and inferior things; for her circle is contained by the circle of Mercury. Mercury's circle, however, is contained by Venus's circle; Venus's circle is contained by the Sun's circle; the Sun's circle is contained by Mars's circle; Mars's circle is contained by Jupiter's circle; Jupiter's circle is contained by Saturn's circle; Saturn's circle is contained by the circle of the fixed stars, beyond which the astrologer has no business getting involved, even though it seemed otherwise to certain people, the issue of which I do not intend to dispute here.

For you see that the Moon at the New Moon appears small, slender, and little; then her light is increased, and it seems that she grows little by little, until her whole body is illuminated from the side we see, and she is in the fullness of her light. Then her light is decreased little by little, and step by step, until it goes down to nothing. So do bodies act, both rational and non-rational, and all vegetable things. For see how men are born: they are increased and grow, until they are perfected in their determinate size, then they are decreased, and begin likewise to decline, and they decline until their life is finished, and so do the rest of things. Whence the Moon is always to be put as a significatrix of every matter and every beginning, and every nativity; and her good condition is the good condition of every matter; and her bad condition is the bad condition of every matter. And it is her virtue alone, and only her power, that even if the Lord of the Ascendant or another significator of some matter were impeded, indeed so that it could not do or perfect what it ought, and she were found to be strong, nevertheless the matter will be perfected. For she is the governess of all matters,

---

[69] See the 143rd Consideration.
[70] *Speciebus.*
[71] *Specierum.*
[72] *Elementata.*

and is the bearer of the virtues of all the planets toward planets, namely one to the other, indeed since she receives the disposition of one planet, and carries it away to another. And it seemed to certain people that she herself always does that. Of which opinion was the tyrant Ezzelino da Romano, namely that when she is separating from one planet, she receives its virtue, and carries it to another, and commits it to the one which she encounters first.[73] And it seemed to certain people that Sahl had said the same thing[74]–but Sahl's intention was not absolute. For he (with whom I agree) believed that the Moon would carry what was committed to her, and if it was not committed to her, she would not carry anything to any [planet]. For the Moon, when she is joined to some planet who receives her, then the planet commits its disposition to her, and she carries it with her and commits it to the one whom she first encounters in one of its own strengths, and not to another. According to this a planet does not give something in a place in which it promised nothing.

THE 10ᵀᴴ CONSIDERATION is that you look for the helping or harming fixed stars (about which it will be spoken in the Treatise on revolutions in its own place and time), which have much work to do concerning judgments, and they sometimes lead the astrologer into error.

THE 11ᵀᴴ CONSIDERATION is to give attention to, and consider, the malefic planets, and see what they would signify. For Saturn and Mars, as I told you above, are naturally malefics. Saturn for instance, on account of the excessive cold, Mars on account of the excessive heat–holding sway and ruling in them: not that either of them is in truth hot or cold, but they have that in their virtue, and it is their effect; and because they signify evil, and detriment, and impediment in matters, unless the malefics were to receive the significator or the Moon by domicile or by exaltation, or by two of their lesser dignities; or the malefics themselves were significators–because then they hold back all their malice from him whom they receive, nor do they impede him, from whatever aspect they were to aspect (better, however, from a trine aspect, or a sextile). If indeed they did not receive, their malice is made greater, and all the more strongly if they were to aspect from the opposition or a square aspect. If for example it were a trine aspect, or a sextile, even if without reception, they will then impede less. However, Sahl seems to want to say[75] that the malefics hold back their own

---

[73] See Bonatti's comment about Ezzelino in Tr. 3, Part 2, Ch. 14.
[74] Bonatti may be thinking the first of Sahl's *50 Judgments*. Below, Bonatti will draw on many of these Judgments.
[75] Judgment 2.

malice if they were to aspect by a trine or sextile aspect;[76] but his intention was that they impede less: he did not however say that their malice would be held back entirely.

THE 12TH CONSIDERATION[77] is to look at the benefics, and to see what they would signify. For Jupiter and Venus are naturally benefics, and are temperate, and because of this they are said to be apart from all malice, because they harm no one unless perhaps sometimes accidentally (which does not happen from their intention, and rarely happens). For they imprint with their own temperament, and they always strive to help what is their own and not their own with success, whether they receive or not (better, however, if they were to receive)– and the trine aspect or the sextile is better, and more useful than the square; and the square is better than the opposition.

THE 13TH CONSIDERATION is to view the Sun, and the things signified by him, because he is said to be a benefic, and that is namely by aspect–by whatever sort of aspect it was–unless it is by the opposition. But by the corporal conjunction evil is effected, because then he is said to burn up and make unfortunate every star, unless the star were in the *kasmīmī*[78] of the Sun, as was said above. Because then it is in the heart of the Sun, and every star in the heart of the Sun is made strong.[79]

THE 14TH CONSIDERATION is to look at Mercury and the Moon, and to see to which of the planets they are conjoined. Because they signify what *that* one (to which one of them is joined) does. For they are of a convertible nature.

THE 15TH CONSIDERATION is to consider the ways by which the planets imprint into inferior things. And they are two: one good, and the other bad. Because the benefics imprint good naturally, the malefics imprint or bring in evil naturally. Whence you ought always to hope for good when you see the benefics and fear evil when you see the malefics, unless [the factors] discussed above decrease it.

THE 16TH CONSIDERATION is to see whether a planetary significator of some matter is impeded by one of the malefics. Because a planet is not said to be impeded by a malefic unless the malefic projects its rays upon[80] his rays,

---

[76] I.e., without reception.

[77] Mistakenly listed as the 11th in the 1550 edition.

[78] Lat. *Zanum*. This is what is usually known as the condition of *cazimi*, often spoken of as being "in the heart of the Sun," from Ar. كصميمي, "as if in the depth," with connotations of intimacy and inwardness.

[79] In this Consideration, "stars" refers to the planets; when speaking of the fixed stars, Bonatti always specifies them as "the fixed stars."

[80] *Super radios.*

according to the quantity of the orbs of their light. After [the malefic] projects its light (whether [it projects] its rays upon[81] the light, or its rays [to] the planet), it is said to be an impeded planet until the malefic transits him. And Sahl said[82] that after the malefic planet were to transit the planet whom it was impeding, by one full degree, the planet is said to be freed from the malefic. But to me it seems that after the malefic has transited him by 1', the planet may be said to be freed, and to have escaped, because [the malefic] cannot introduce anything after that unless it is fear.

Moreover, he will introduce greater fear when he has transited him by only 1' than when he has transited him by 1°. Still, however, the fear which the malefic introduces (when he has transited the planet by only 1') is such that it does not seem to him (whose matter it is), that he could escape, nor however without a little thread of hope. As an example of this, someone who wanted to go to a battle posed the question whether or not he would return safe and sound from the fight or not. And the Ascendant was Gemini, 13°; and Mercury was in Aquarius by 7° 54' in the 9th, joined to Saturn, who was likewise in Aquarius by 7° 53'. And Mercury was separating from Saturn (who was the Lord of the house of death), already by 1'. Therefore it seemed that he ought to have died in the battle on account of the conjunction which [Mercury] was making with Saturn in the eighth degree of Aquarius; whence he was in danger of death, and feared as though with the ultimate fear, and believed he would be killed by his enemies. And he had been pursued by them so that it did not seem he would be able to escape. And often they had their hands on him; ultimately however he escaped from them after practically losing hope, because he did not believe he could escape. And this happened to him because of Mercury, who had already been separated from Saturn. And Sahl said[83] that if the malefic planet who were impeding some business, were cadent from the Ascendant, so that it does not aspect it, it does not impede, but he will introduce only fear.

THE 17TH CONSIDERATION is to see whether a planetary significator is safe, indeed so that it is not impeded by any of the malefics, and [that] one of the benefics projects its own rays or light upon[84] his rays or upon[85] his light. Because then the planet is said to be safe until the benefic transits by 1'; and it signifies the perfection of a matter. After it has transited him by 1', it is not

---

[81] *Super lumen.*
[82] Judgment 4.
[83] Judgment 4.
[84] *Super radios.*
[85] *Super lumen.*

perfected, nor does the matter send [anything] to him but hope, just as a malefic does not send [anything] but fear, as I said. And the hope which the benefic gives is such that the querent believes that the matter will be perfected for him, and it seems to him that it is settled concerning the perfection of his matter, not however without the rendering of some kind of doubt. For example, a certain question was posed concerning a certain difficult business deal, whether the matter would be perfected or not. And the Ascendant was Scorpio, 17°; and Mars was in Taurus, 12° 13'; and Venus in Capricorn, 12° 14'. And truly, Venus was joined to Mars by a trine aspect, and she was receiving him from her own domicile, and Mars was receiving her from his exaltation; and it seemed to the querent, and to all those handling the business deal, that it ought to have been perfected on account of the aspect of full friendship. And they stood fast in their hope until Venus transited the aspect of Mars by one full degree. In the end however, the matter was destroyed, on account of the fact that Venus had already transited Mars by 1' by the time the question was made.

It can sometimes be that a matter would be perfected in such a case, but not without great obstacles, and great labor, and great complications, and much effort and inconvenience. And Sahl said[86] that if the benefic were cadent from the Ascendant, so that it did not aspect it, it gives only hope and does not perfect the business.

THE 18TH CONSIDERATION [is] that you consider when a planet is in the angles of the malefics. Because unless a malefic were to receive him, he is said to be in evils, and in distress, and tribulations, just like a man whom some people had attacked, and on whom they perpetrated an insult, whom no one helps, who fights and defends himself from many people; and so is one who strives and works against fortune, and everything goes adversely for him; and so is one who fell into a whirlpool and does not know how to swim, however he moves his hands and feet so that at some time he reaches the shore and escapes, even if it does not happen all the time.

And a planet is said to be in the angles of a malefic when the malefic is in one sign, and the planet is in the fourth [sign] from it, or in the seventh [sign] or tenth [sign], like if the malefic were in Aries, and the other planet were in Cancer, or in Libra, or in Capricorn: it is said to be in its angles.[87] You may understand the same about the corporal conjunction. But if it were to receive [the other planet], it does not impede because reception breaks all malice, as is

---

[86] Judgment 4.

[87] In other words, when a planet is in square or opposition to a malefic by whole sign aspects.

said elsewhere. Indeed after (as was said) he were to transit him by one full minute, the planet is said to have escaped from the danger of that malefic, and from its impediment. And after he were to transit him by 1°, he is said to be safe, because [the malefic] cannot do any evil to him, even if he brings some fear.[88] And do not forget this which I tell you: because they could be useful to you, as much in nativities as in questions, and in the inceptions of all matters.

THE 19TH CONSIDERATION is that you should look at the Moon when she is void in course: because then she signifies impediment, and that the matter the question was about, or which is begun, or which is being handled [or discussed], will not come to a good end, and the matter will be annulled, and it will not come to be nor be completed for the one wishing to do it; and that the querent will return from it empty-handed and likewise disgraced and impeded.

THE 20TH CONSIDERATION is that you look to see if the Moon or a significator is joined to one of the planets, because then it signifies that it is going to be. Whence you must consider whether he to whom the Moon (or the significator of the matter or question) is joined, receives [the significator] or the Moon: for then it signifies the full completion and perfection of the matter, and its good and praiseworthy end—I say this if the receiver were a benefic. If however it did not receive, and the Moon or the Lord or significator of the matter were to commit disposition to it, nevertheless however the matter will be perfected. But if it were a malefic, even if the Moon or the significator commits disposition to it, and reception did not intervene, it will not be perfected—and evil and detriment will be introduced into their sides.[89] If however it were to receive, nor were it otherwise impeded, it signifies the perfection of the matter, even if with labor and obstacles and weariness.

THE 21ST CONSIDERATION is that you should see from which of the planets the Moon is being separated, because it signifies that it already was and is past; for if she is being separated from a benefic, it signifies good which already was; if indeed she is being separated from a malefic, it signifies evil which already was. Whence if you wish to judge about that which already was, and it is past, you can speak about it in accordance with how you were to see the Moon to be separated from one of the planets.

THE 22ND CONSIDERATION is that you consider to whom (from among the planets) the Moon is conjoined, because it signifies that it is present. Whence if

---

[88] So the whole sign aspect will *at least* bring distress and fear; but no serious harm will result unless they are applying by actual degrees.

[89] *Interponens partes suas.* By "part," Bonatti means the parties or sides involved in some matter. He sometimes uses this term in Tr. 6, especially in horaries involving conflict.

you wished to judge something about a present matter, it is necessary for you to consider to whom the Moon is now joined, degree by degree, or by less than one degree, and you ought to judge good or evil according to the one to whom she is joined.

THE 23RD CONSIDERATION is that you look to the Moon to see to whom she is then joined–however, so that her conjunction [to it] is not yet completed. Because it signifies what is going to be. Whence if it were necessary for you to judge about a matter which does not yet exist, and it is hoped that it will come into act, you must pay attention to him to whom the Moon then wished to be joined; and you ought to judge good or evil according to the significations of him to whom you saw her wanting to join.

THE 24TH CONSIDERATION is that you look to see if a planetary significator were in its own descension, because then it signifies the impediment of what-ever matter belonged to the significator–and distress and sorrow because of it. And if the question were about a prison which someone feared, it signifies his falling into it, and likewise disgrace and detriment. And if it were about an incarcerated person, it signifies his long stay in the prison, and a [legal] fiction[90] in it, more than the incarcerated person believes.

THE 25TH CONSIDERATION is that you consider whether the planetary signifi-cator of some matter is retrograde, or stationary in its first station: because then it signifies evil, and impediment, and discord, and diversity and contradiction, and a repetition in evil, and disobedience, and turning back to evil from whatever the reversion was, and in a bad direction.[91] But in its station it does not signify as much evil as in retrogradation, because retrogradation signifies a present evil, and a past one which which is still virtually present, and a future one which is already as though in the process of becoming. Indeed the first station signifies evil which is already complete, according to incomplete time.[92]

THE 26TH CONSIDERATION is that you see whether a planetary significator is in its second station, because then it signifies impediment and evil which already was and is past. However, certain people said that the second station signifies what direct motion does–but that is to be understood according to a certain manner of speaking, just as it is said about someone who was sick, and he is

---

[90] *Fictionem.* Usually Bonatti uses *fingo* in relation to enemies who falsely pretend (*se fingunt*) to be the querent's friends, but it also pertains to counterfeiting and fictitious legal assumptions, so I take it to be something sinister like that.

[91] *Reiterationem...in mala parte.*

[92] *Secundum tempus imperfectum.* Coley omits this last phrase. I am not sure exactly what Bonatti means by it.

already getting better, that he is already freed and healthy–but that is not true pure and simple, even if it is near the truth. For just as the first station does not signify as much evil as retrogradation does, so the second station does not signify as much good as direct motion does.

THE 27TH CONSIDERATION is that you see whether the malefic planets are significators of some matter, or of some work, or of some beginning, or of some nativity, or of one of the things which happen every day, or which pass through the hands of men, because if they were to signify evil, they will signify it more greatly; and if they were to signify good, they will signify it to be diminished, and incomplete, and with sorrow and distress, and difficulty and oppression, so that he whose business it was, will hardly believe that it will be perfected for him, unless perhaps the malefics themselves are of a very good condition and well disposed.

THE 28TH CONSIDERATION is to see if the planetary significator of some matter were slow in course: for then it prolongs the effecting of the quaesited matter. And if it were the beginning of some building, it will be prolonged, and its completion will be delayed, so that it will hardly or never be perfected. And if it were a promise made to someone, what was promised will be delayed, and will hardly be perfected, or most slowly, for the one to whom the promise was made. And if threats were made to someone, their effects will not hasten, or [they will be] bad promises.[93] They even delay matters if the significators were in Sagittarius, in Capricorn, in Aquarius, and in Pisces, whether or not their Lords (namely Jupiter and Saturn) were slow; but if they were slow, they postpone more. If indeed they were in Aries or Scorpio, they postpone less than in the aforesaid signs. If however they were in Leo, they hasten. If for instance [they were] in Taurus or Libra, they hasten more. If in Gemini or Virgo, they hasten more so again than in the other signs.

THE 29TH CONSIDERATION is that you pay attention to whether the Moon is joined corporally or by aspect to one of the planets, and her conjunction was complete, minute by minute. Because then it signifies that it is present (concerning the matter). And when she has transited that minute, you must see to which of the planets she is joined: because he will signify that which ought to come of the matter. You will even look at the planet from which the Moon were then separated before she was joined to him to whom (it was said) [she was joined] right away, minute by minute. Because he signifies that which had already been concerning the matter.

---

[93] In other words, even threats made will not be realized.

THE 30ᵀᴴ CONSIDERATION is that you look to see when a planetary significator or the Moon has already transited the twenty-ninth degree of the sign in
which it is, and has touched its thirtieth degree, especially if it has transited one
minute of the same degree: because then there will be no strength for it in that
sign, but there will be in the following one. Whence if it had first signified
something bad, it would not have harmed the one which it seemed it ought to
harm, like if some house threatened to fall, it would not wound the one who
had left it and had already put one foot on the threshold of the door, and had
the other advancing beyond the threshold itself, quickly leaving, and then the
house fell down. And if it had signified some good for someone, it would not
profit him unless it is like someone who has thrown a snare toward some bird
and touched the feathers of its tail, but did not catch him. Whence Sahl said[94] if
a planet or the Moon were in the twenty-ninth degree of some sign, that its
strength exists thus far in the sign in which it is; because he did not yet transit
the twenty-ninth degree entirely, and in the degree which is before it, and which
is after it.

THE 31ˢᵀ CONSIDERATION is that you note, when one planet seeks the conjunction of another, if it were next to the end of the sign in which he himself, or
it whose conjunction he seeks, is; that [the second planet] leaves from that sign
before the conjunction is perfected; and see if he is joined to it in the following
sign to which he is changed: then the purpose is perfected if the planet gives
him something in the sign in which it is joined to him (this is if reception
intervened)–unless he or it to whom he wishes to be joined, is first joined to
another (because then the purpose is annulled, and is not perfected). Even [see]
if it is again joined to the other to whom he first wanted to be joined after he
was separated from the one to whom he was joined when he was changed from
the said sign, since the other imposed itself before the first conjunction could be
perfected.[95] Nor should you forget [this]: because a corporal conjunction will
prohibit an aspect, and cuts it off, but an aspect will neither prohibit nor cut off
a corporal conjunction.[96]

THE 32ᴺᴰ CONSIDERATION is that you look to see, if a malefic planet were
the significator of some matter, what kind of condition it [had]: because if it
were good, it will be good concerning the matter. If however it were bad, it will
be bad concerning the matter. Sarcinator said something just like this in the

---

[94] Judgment 15.
[95] See Tr. 3, Part 2, Ch. 12-13, 17.
[96] This last point is an important one for understanding the various ways that matter may be
perfected or not.

Pentedeca: a malefic planet, when it is oriental[97] in its domicile or exaltation, and is not joined to a malefic who impedes him, is better and more dignified than a retrograde and impeded benefic.

THE 33RD CONSIDERATION is that you see whether some malefic is the significator of some matter and is joined to another malefic who impedes him; or the Lord of the Ascendant or the Moon were joined to him by an evil aspect, namely by a square or opposition: for the malefic perfects the purpose but does not make it arrive to a good end–rather it will destroy it after it seemed to be arranged and is believed to be perfected. But if the malefic who impeded were lighter, so that it sought the conjunction of the significator, it will impede less than if the significator were seeking the conjunction of the malefic who impedes; so that it will be worse if the significator pushes than if it itself is pushed.[98]

THE 34TH CONSIDERATION is that you look to see in questions or in nativities, or in any other matters about which you have to judge, whether the significator of the business being handled is a malefic and is the Lord of the Ascendant, and is himself in the Ascendant, direct and of good condition. Because if it were so, it perfects the matter, and makes it arrive to a good end; and even if it is not the significator, nor is it the Lord of the Ascendant, and it is in the Ascendant, and the Ascendant were its exaltation, it will put down all its malice and will be held back from an evil impediment. Impeded, it increases its malice and its harmfulness and its contrariety is multiplied, and it will try in every way to destroy the business.

THE 35TH CONSIDERATION is that you look to see whether a malefic planet is in signs similar to it: because then it reduces its malice, and it is just like one who has what he wants, because then he is found to be of good will, and more upright, and more merciful, and less malicious. Like when Saturn is in Capricorn or Aquarius or Libra, or in a cold sign (and especially if he had some dignity there), and like when Mars is in Aries, or Scorpio, or in Capricorn, or in a hot sign (and especially if he had some dignity there), because then he perfects it. If indeed Saturn were in a hot sign, outside of his dignities, or Mars [were] in a cold sign, outside of his dignities, it will be bad, nor is the purpose perfected, just like a mixture of water with oil is not easily accomplished, nor do they embrace each other. If indeed they were of a good condition and well disposed

---

[97] Coley incorrectly reads "strong" instead of "oriental."
[98] This is based on Sahl, Judgment 19. Here "pushing" refers to the influence being transferred or applied to the slower planet.

(as I said), they will then be capable of being mixed in well, and they perfect the purpose just like a conjunction of water with wine, or with honey or with milk.[99]

THE 36TH CONSIDERATION is that you consider, when the malefics signify impediment, whether the benefics will aspect them by a trine or sextile aspect: because then they reduce their impediment, and much more strongly so if [the benefics] were to receive [the malefics].

THE 37TH CONSIDERATION is to see, if the benefics were significators, whether the malefics aspect them from the opposition or from a square aspect, because then they reduce their fortune and goodness.

THE 38TH CONSIDERATION is that you consider, if the benefics were significators, if they are cadent from the angles, or from the Ascendant (so that they do not aspect it), and are retrograde: because then they will be impeded, and will be practically like malefics unless they are received.

THE 39TH CONSIDERATION is that you look to see if the planet who was the significator is received: because if it were a benefic, what it signifies will be better than otherwise; if however it were a malefic, its impediment will be less; it will even impede (if he ought to impede some [planet]), after he was received.

THE 40TH CONSIDERATION is that you look to see if a malefic planet were peregrine (whether it was the significator or not): that is, that he is not in any of his own dignities. Because then his malice is made greater–and likewise the evil and impediment which he signified. And if he were in his own dignities (namely in domicile or exaltation or in [his] bound), his impediment is decreased and he restrains his own malice. In [his] triplicity and in [his] face, he restrains it less. In *haym*, however, less again.

THE 41ST CONSIDERATION is that you look to see if a malefic planet were the significator of some matter or some beginning, and he were in his domicile or exaltation, or bound, or triplicity, and in the angles [or] the succeedents: because then he is said to be strong like a benefic.

THE 42ND CONSIDERATION is that you pay attention [to see] if a benefic were the significator or were to offer its aid[100] to one of the planets, and were in a domicile in which it had none of the aforesaid dignities: because then its good and fortune is decreased. And if it were in one of its stated dignities, it perfects the matter and increases its strength and good, and its fortune is made greater.

---

[99] See Sahl, Judgment 21.

[100] *Praebuerit suum adminiculum.* I do not know if this is supposed to be a technical phrase. It may be that Bonatti is quoting another authority (like Sahl) without telling us; or, this is shorthand for the usual formula of "aspecting by a sextile or trine aspect," perhaps with reception, *etc.*

THE 43ᴿᴰ CONSIDERATION is to see if the benefics and malefics were in malign places at the same time, namely in one of the impediments, which I have already told you above and often–that is, in houses [domiciles?] in which they do not have testimony, and [if they] were combust: because then they signify whatever they signify, more weakly; and they signify weak and despicable things. Nor could the benefics signify good, nor the malefics evil, on account of the excess of their weakness. In accordance with which, the Philosopher says there is no strength in signification for a retrograde and combust planet. Whence Sahl said,[101] wherefore when a planet is combust under that rays of the Sun, or is in [the Sun's] opposition, it will be weak: because in that place there is no usefulness, [there is] nothing good for the benefic planets, nor is there any evil for the malefic planets. Because the benefics signify nothing good or by means of good when they are combust; likewise when the malefics are combust they have little or no virtue in signifying evil, and they can introduce less impediment then.

THE 44ᵀᴴ CONSIDERATION is that you look to see if the planetary significator (whether a benefic or malefic) were in its own domicile, or in its exaltation, or its triplicity, or in its bound, or in its face (but face is not of as much virtue as are the other aforesaid dignities). Whence it is necessary that it will be helped by another dignity, namely by light[102] or *haym*. Because then the malefic is restrained from its malice just like a vicious horse is restrained from its viciousness[103] by a strong bridle; and whatever evil is in it, is converted into good; and a benefic fortifies, and increases good. And even if it should seem like something to be wondered at, still the majority of the philosophers swear to this, and I have seen it come out this way in my own times. Whence you ought to consider all these things which I have told you under this heading, and thus you could judge truly about it; for I have not found it to disappoint.

THE 45ᵀᴴ CONSIDERATION is that you look to see if the malefics are in the angles of the Ascendant, and impede one of the planets by a square aspect or from the opposition: because then they will impede and afflict more and their harm will be greater; and especially if the malefics were in a stronger place than is the planet whom they impede. If indeed they were to aspect by a trine or

---

[101] This is a combination of Judgments 38-40.
[102] This is undoubtedly version (a), being in one's "own *light*," that is to say, being in *halb*: a diurnal planet in the day above the earth and below it in the night; or a nocturnal planet above the earth in the night and below it in the day. See Introduction.
[103] "Vicious" (*vitiosus*) should be considered in its older sense of being bad and defective, which could include, but is not restricted to, violence and destruction.

sextile aspect, they will be restrained from evil and their malice is decreased, and likewise their impediment.

THE 46TH CONSIDERATION is to look at the planet who is the significator [and see] whether it is a benefic or a malefic: because a benefic always signifies fortune naturally; a malefic however, always signifies evil naturally, which happens to it on account of the overflowing of malignancy in its nature. Whence it is necessary for you to pay attention to the places of the planets from the Ascendant in which they are: for if a planet were in its own light, or in its own *haym*,[104] or in one of its dignities, or in a good place from the Ascendant, it signifies good. If however it were a benefic, it signifies greater good.

THE 47TH CONSIDERATION is that you consider whether a significator is in its own light: namely, a diurnal planet in the day above the earth, and in the night below the earth; and a nocturnal planet in the night above the earth, and in the day below the earth.[105] [But] were a nocturnal planetary significator of some matter in the day above the earth; or a diurnal planet in the night [below the earth], or were the significator peregrine (namely that it did not have dignity in the place in which it was), or were it cadent from the Ascendant (so that it did not aspect it); or cadent from the angles: for then it is impeded, and it impedes that which it signifies; nor can it perfect it.

THE 48TH CONSIDERATION is that you see if a malefic planet is a significator and threatens evil, whether Jupiter aspects him or is joined to him by his own body: because then [Jupiter] will break the malice, and will turn his nature into good, of whatever sort the malefic was. For so great is his goodness and strength in the good. Because he breaks all the malice of Saturn, and turns it into good. Whence if Saturn does not give good in that place, nor would he perfect the matter which he promised, Jupiter makes him give and perfect the matter, whether Saturn wanted to or not–unless Jupiter were himself impeded by fall or combustion or retrogradation: for then he helps, but does not wholly perfect the matter. Indeed Venus breaks the malice of Mars on account of the excessive friendship which is found between them, unless the matter is very difficult (as are the clashes of arms and wars, and sheddings of blood). However

---

104 Here Bonatti seems to distinguishes "own light" from *haym*, so it is hard to know what exactly he means.

105 These positions of strength are identical to *halb*; now Bonatti lists the corresponding positions of weakness. This may be an elaboration of Sahl's example of a planet being "in its own light": "A planet is said to be in its own light, like Mars (who is nocturnal) were a significator at night; and Saturn (who is diurnal) is said to be in his light in the day" (*Introduct.* §5.16)

she cannot break the malice of Saturn without the aid of Jupiter, for then he breaks the malice of Saturn like she breaks the malice of Mars. Because Saturn does not applaud Venus in any way, because Saturn is slow, Venus is quick; he is heavy, she light; he rejoices in lamentation, she in taking delight.[106]

THE 49TH CONSIDERATION is that you consider whether one of the malefics is the significator of someone, and if he is joined to another of the malefics: because if he were to signify any good,[107] the good is destroyed. If indeed he were to signify some evil, it will be increased, and will come to be worse, or will be changed into some greater evil, like when pain made around the navel is changed into dry dropsy. If however it were joined to a benefic who received him, or he it, then the evil will be led away into good. But if some reception did not intervene, the evil is not wholly cancelled but is mitigated, so that it is less, in accordance with how the benefic is disposed, since it is possible that it would be decreased so much that it will seem to harm only moderately.

THE 50TH CONSIDERATION is that you look at the Lord of the Ascendant of some matter, and the Moon, to see if they (or one of them) were impeded by the malefics (namely by conjunction or by opposition or a square aspect): the matter is impeded without the aspect of a benefic. While if a benefic (namely Jupiter or Venus or the Sun or the Moon) were then to aspect him, the malice of the impeding malefic is dissolved, and he whose significator was the Lord of the Ascendant or the Moon, is freed (if some danger were threatening him) from the fear of the malefic's being let in, even if the aspect was a square[108] (provided that it is with reception). While if the benefic were to aspect without reception from a square aspect or from the opposition, or a malefic from a trine or sextile without reception, then it will be possible that he whose significator was the Lord of the Ascendant or the Moon would be freed from the impediment which seems to threaten him, but it will be converted into an evil that is equally bad, or a little less, so that it will not seem as though his liberation was useful.

THE 51ST CONSIDERATION is that you look to see whether the planetary significator of some matter is cadent from an angle, and from the Ascendant,

---

[106] Bonatti has an interesting choice of words: Saturn does not *applaud* Venus, i.e., show a certain respect or appreciation for her. But why would he show it for Jupiter? Perhaps Bonatti is implying that their slowness and heaviness makes them a better match, as when two powerful people who do not like each other still respect each other's power.
[107] I.e., by signifying a good thing by rulership, like if he were the Lord of the 2nd (wealth) or the 5th (children).
[108] *Tetragonus*. This is one of several times when Bonatti suddenly switches from his usual Latin term to a Greek-derived one, and vice versa.

nor is it in one of its own dignities, nor in its joy: because then it signifies every evil, and every doubt [or fear]; and no usefulness, and nothing good, and no hope, will be in the matter; and such a planet, so disposed, could signify nothing praiseworthy.

THE 52ND [CONSIDERATION] is when the three inferiors (namely Venus, Mercury, and the Moon) go out from under the rays, and come to the evening place,[109] namely so they appear in the evening after the setting of the Sun: because before they go out from under the rays of the Sun and are elongated from him by 12°, any strength of theirs will be weak–and even of the others, so that a benefic could not particularly be of use; likewise a malefic could not particularly harm. Whence if [it were] a benefic, it would provide advantage with difficulty and slowly, so that with great labor, with great obstacles, and great complications, the advantage will come. And if it were a malefic, what it signifies will appear slowly. Indeed among the superiors (which are Saturn, Jupiter, and Mars), these things happen when they go out from under the rays of the Sun, as they rise in the morning before the Sun, and appear before his rising.[110]

THE 53RD CONSIDERATION is that you look to see whether a planetary significator is under the rays of the Sun, because then it will be weak and of practically no strength in any matter; however the malefics will be somewhat stronger in evil than the benefics in good, even if not by very much. For then the planet is said to be under the rays of the Sun when there are exactly 12° or less between itself and the Sun, and more than 16'. Because when there are exactly 16' or less between the planet and the Sun, it is said to be strong, because it is then in *kasmīmī* or in the heart of the Sun, just as I told you above. Indeed if there were more than 12° and less than 15° between the planet and the Sun, it is said to be going out from under its rays.

THE 54TH CONSIDERATION is that you look to see whether a superior planet is elongated from the Sun by 12°, going toward the morning rising-place,[111], just as much as an inferior planet is, and itself direct, going toward the evening setting-place[112]–because then it is said to be strong.[113] Indeed, after it was

---

[109] *Ortum* (signifying rising and setting places of the Sun), as opposed to *locum* (signifying places in the zodiac).

[110] This whole paragraph refers to making a morning or evening appearance with the Sun, which in Hellenistic astrology makes a planet's power more dramatic.

[111] *Ad ortum matutinum.*

[112] *Ad ortum vespertinum.*

[113] In other words, the "morning place" is the position whereby the superiors rise before the Sun when he separates from them; the "evening place" is the position where by the inferiors

elongated from him by 15°, so that it appears from under the rays of the Sun, it is said to be stronger than it could be in every matter, like someone is who has left a battle, all of his enemies having been completely overcome, and he is resting, and rejoices in his victory; nor does he fear anyone else who will rise up against him, or who will resist him in anything; for he is then cheerful, of good spirit, of a good disposition, blessed in every way.

When however the Sun pursues the three superiors, and there are less than 15° between them and him, their weakness is said to be increased up until there are only 7° between them and the Sun; and after there are less than 7° between them and the Sun, up until they are in the heart of the Sun, they are said to be in the ultimate weakness. Indeed the weakness of the three inferiors is the contrary of this. For it is said to be increased when they pursue the Sun, and there are from 15° to 7° between them and the Sun; and from 7 [degrees] up until they are in the heart of the Sun, they are said to be in the ultimate weakness.[114]

THE 55TH CONSIDERATION is that you look to see whether a planetary significator is peregrine, because then it signifies that he whose significator he is (whether it is in a nativity or in a question, or in the beginning of some matter) will be clever, astute, malicious—for he will know how to do good and evil, and how to advance cleverly in all actions which he wished; however, his intention will be more inclined toward evil than to good. And if it were in one of its own greater dignities (namely in domicile or exaltation), and it were direct, and were in a good place from the Ascendant (in the tenth or in the eleventh) or in some aspect of friendship to the Ascendant, then it will signify the good effecting of the quaesited matters or undertakings, and the good mind and good will of the native or querent or quaesited. If however it were in one of its own lesser dignities, its signification will be less than this.

THE 56TH CONSIDERATION is that you look to see, if the planetary significator of some matter committed its own disposition to some planet, whether the receiver of its disposition [were] oriental or occidental. Because if it were oriental, and of the inferiors, and it were direct (or it were occidental and of the

---

set after the Sun when they separate from him. The bad positions for each of these groups of planets is the opposite (see succeeding paragraph). Bonatti is interested in that first appearance or *phasis*.

[114] The basis of this Consideration is that the Hellenistic astrologers wanted to know whether, within seven days before or after the nativity, a planet could make a morning or evening appearance just outside the Sun's beams. The required distance from the Sun needed for making such an appearance was standardized at 15°, the outer limit of the Sun's "beams." Since the Sun moves at about 1° per day, 7° generally allows the planet to be able to make such an appearance. This seems to be the basis for the sunbeams/combustion distinction.

superiors), and there were less than 20° between it and the Sun, it will be weak, as Sarcinator says, and what it judged or showed is not perfected. For then it is impeded more by such an impediment, which is like an impediment by which a man is impeded who is already beginning to get sick, so that the illness has already prevailed so much that the sick person is thought to have fallen:[115] he practically cannot help himself without the aid of another; and like a building which has already started to go to ruin, nor is there anyone who would protect it so it does not fall down. And by how much more the planet is far from the Sun, it impedes by that much less. And if it were oriental and were of the superiors, or were occidental and were of the inferiors, nor were retrograde, it will be strong and well-fitted to perfect what it indicates, just like a man who was sick, and now is wholly freed, and has resumed all his powers; and just like a building which had already fallen, and now is restored, and newly raised, and improved in all of its parts; thus it is with all of the aforesaid planets so disposed.

THE 57TH CONSIDERATION is that you look to see whether a planetary significator is in the 8th from the Ascendant: because if it were found in it, and it were a benefic, even if it did not do evil, it will not do good. And if it were a malefic, it will accomplish more evil than in any of the other places in the whole figure, and its malice will be magnified. And if it were a question of one going to war, do not counsel him to go then, even if it were a benefic, because evil—namely death, or at least capture–is always to be suspected, for it is the place of darkness and death. If however it were a malefic, you could judge death for him, unless it were separating then from the Lord of the eighth: because then it could signify wounds or blows, or an occasion why it seemed he could die, even if by chance he could escape. And if it were some journey, and expecially a long one, you could judge capture, or at least the greatest fear in the journey. Always understand this if it would be separating from the Lord of the eighth, and understand likewise that a malefic so disposed as I said will always accomplish more evil than fortune.

THE 58TH CONSIDERATION is that you look to see whether a planetary significator is fixed in the sign in which it were found. And Sahl said[116] that a planet is not said to be fixed in a sign unless it had traveled through 5° in it.

---

[115] The verb *iaceo* also has connotations of lying dead or having been killed in battle. Also, see Bonatti's use of this in Tr. 9, Part 2, Ch. 2, in the section *On the knowledge of the* al-kadukhadāh, where he makes Dorotheus allow this *phasis* to make a planet the *hilāj* and the *al-kadukhadāh*.
[116] Judgment 44. Sahl says *firmetur*, "made firm."

But[117] to me it seems that after a planet has traveled through one full degree of a sign, that it is firmly in it; he however spoke toward greater clarity, and said that a planet is not said to be cadent from the Ascendant unless it is elongated by it by 5°. For example, the Ascendant was 9° Aries, and a planet was in the fifth degree of Aries. Ptolemy says about this (and many other sages say) that such a planet is in the angle–with all of whom I agree. Indeed certain others wanted it that the planet would be said to be in an angle when he is in the degree of the Ascendant itself, or by one 1° ahead of it, or 2° after.[118] But their concern was with the revolutions of years, and because they wanted to be certain they could not be deceived in any matter. I however have proven that a planet is in an angle up until near the full amount of 5° beyond the cusp of any angle: for, while in a certain year I was investigating the revolution of that year, I found Mars in the fifth degree beyond the angle of the earth [the 4th], and he was in Capricorn, and his latitude was southern, and it signified the killing of the Roman Emperor; and it signified that for him then, for he was then in Grosseto, and I in Forli; and Pandolfo de Fasanella[119] and Tibaldi Franciscus,[120] and many others of their secretaries, were found to have formed a conspiracy to kill him,[121] and none of their astrologers discovered this because they did not believe that Mars was in the angle: for he had transited the cusp of the angle by 4° 58', according to their opinion. Indeed, after a planet is elongated from the cusp or from the line of some angle by 5°, it is said to be cadent from the angle.[122]

THE 59TH CONSIDERATION is that you look to see whether a planetary significator is after the line of the angle by 15° and not more; for it is said to be in the angle just as much as he who is directly on the angle, according to which it

---

[117] The remainder of this Consideration is in Bonatti's own voice, not Sahl's (as Coley's edition makes it seem).

[118] I believe that by "ahead of," Bonatti means "in an earlier degree than the cusp's"; by "after," he means "in a later degree than the cusp's." By "beyond" (see the last sentence of this paragraph), he means "in an earlier degree than the cusp's, i.e., having already passed beyond it by primary motion. See my Introduction.

[119] Pandolfo de Fasanella was then the vicar general of Tuscany.

[120] Lat. *Theobaldus Franciscus.* The Latin does not have a comma, and Van Cleve (pp. 490-91) reports that Tibaldi Franciscus was the *podestà* of Parma. But Boncompagni places a comma between the names and reports this as though they are two men: Teobaldo and Francesco.

[121] Bonatti is referring to Pope Innocent IV's plot against Frederick in 1245, which was uncovered by Count Richard of Caserta in early 1246. Bonatti may be referring to his own location because it suggests that he was unable to warn the Emperor. Grosseto is an Italian province in Tuscany. See van Cleve (1972), pp. 490-91.

[122] In other words, by primary motion it has moved away from the angle by 5° or more.

seemed to Sahl.[123] From thence afterwards he said that it was not in the angle; and he said there would be no strength for him in the angle beyond the fifteenth degree after the angle. For example, the Ascendant was the fourth degree of Taurus; up to [Taurus's] end was after the angle; but whichever of the planets was from the fourth degree of Taurus up to the nineteenth degree of it, was in the angle; indeed, whichever one was beyond the nineteenth degree, was not in the angle.

Indeed Ptolemy seems to want to mean, even if he does not say it expressly, that every planet which is before an angle by 5° and after it up to the twenty-fifth degree, is in the angle. Sahl wanted to remove the worry that a great elongation of the planet from an angle would impede [its] business.[124] Ptolemy (from whom I do not dissent) seems to want it that no part of some house remain devoid of virtue. It seems to me, though, nor do I believe in vain, that every planet which is in some house, is said to be, and is, in that house in which it is found, from the beginning of that house up to its end. And therefore I say in a house, and not in a sign, because one house sometimes encloses more than one sign, sometimes less than one sign. For it would seem ridiculous that some part of a house should remain closed off[125] or devoid of virtue.

THE 60TH CONSIDERATION is that you look to see whether a planetary significator is in a fixed sign, or a common or movable one: because in a fixed sign it signifies the fixity and stability and durability of the matter undertaken or begun, or about which a question was made. When it is in a common sign, it signifies change, and repetition of a matter already undertaken or to be begun, or about which there was a question, and that the matter will be dissolved and begun again, or that another matter will be commingled with it, and will connect to it; or something like an alteration or repetition will happen with the matter. Whence in matters whose alteration[126] we desire, as are buying, selling and similar actions, we ought to put the planetary significator, and the Moon, or at least one of them, into a common sign. And if it were in a movable sign, it signifies a quick change or alteration of the matter, or of something undertaken, or to be begun, or asked about, or of whatever sort it is—and its quick completion and fast end, whether it signified good or evil.

---

[123] Judgment 45. Sahl gives a similar example, but Bonatti uses his own.
[124] *Negotium.*
[125] Reading *occlusa* for *oclosa.*
[126] Alteration here should be taken in its etymological context of something passing to an "other" (*alter*), just as when buying and selling money and goods pass from one person to another.

Whence in matters whose quick end we desire, we ought to put the significators in movable signs. In matters whose durability and long fixity we desire, we ought to put the significators in fixed signs. In those which whose middling [quality] we desire, we ought to put the significators in common ones. You may always understand the same about the nature of the Moon, if you can ever make it so. And again I repeat to you, that the fixed signs signify fixity, durability and unity [oneness]; the common ones signify plurality; the movable ones, the quickness of change.

THE 61ST CONSIDERATION is that you look to see whether the Lord of the Ascendant (or the Moon) is [corporally] with the Head or Tail of the Dragon: because then it signifies impediment in every matter; and the impediment will come from or out of the cause that is signified by the house in which the conjunction (namely, of the significator or the Moon with the Head or Tail) is. And another conjunction of the Head or Tail does not harm unless [it is] corporal, because they do not have an aspect nor an opposition. And it is worse when the signficator or the Moon goes toward them than when [the significator and the Moon] recede, as is said elsewhere; for when they go toward them, then they signify the ultimate evil, just like what happens to him who is in a ship when it is in danger, and is broken in the sea, because then there is no hope for him. But when they recede from them, it is like when a ship has already been endangered, because one of the navigators can cling to something (namely to a plank or dross[127] and to similar things) which gives him hope of escaping, and sometimes he escapes. And it must be known that when the significator of a matter or the Moon goes toward the Head, its malice is increased; and it is more than when it recedes from it, because its nature is to increase. And when it goes toward the Tail, it is not wholly the extreme malice like when it is separating itself from it, namely less than 1°. From 1° earlier its malice is not so great as it is within that degree, even though it is great; and from one to three, it is said to be less enough; and from three to five, it is said to be again less; and from five to seven, it is said to be small; and from seven up to nine, it is said to be smaller; and from nine to twelve, it is said to be practically none.

THE 62ND CONSIDERATION is that you look to see whether the Moon is void in course: for the voiding of a course signifies that the matter about which it is asked, could hardly or never be perfected or arrive to a good end. And if it were perfected, it will be perfected with labor, and likewise with distress, and sorrow, unless the Lord of the Ascendant or the significator of the matter were of very

---

127 Reading *scoria* for *scorea*.

good condition; because if it were so, even though impeded,[128] it does not destroy the matter entirely. However someone can refrain from taking part in [things] (namely drinking bouts, baths, feasts, and the like) when the Moon is impeded. And likewise [it is good] (especially when she is in Scorpio) to use *annora*,[129] which is a certain oil removing hairs, which in Latin is called a *psilotrum*[130] (however it is commonly called a *sconapotum*[131]).[132]

THE 63RD CONSIDERATION is that you look to see whether the Moon is so far from a conjunction with the malefics, that she does not project her rays upon[133] the rays of a malefic; for if it were so, then it signifies the good eventuating of the matter about which it was asked or which is coming to be; and better than that is if she projects her rays upon[134] the rays of some benefic; and much more strongly if the Lord of the Ascendant or the significator of the matter were of good condition. If however it were not well disposed, the good that is signified will be decreased; however it will not be wholly destroyed, for indeed some good part of it would remain.

THE 64TH CONSIDERATION is that you look to see whether the Moon is in Cancer, or in Taurus, or in Sagittarius, or in Pisces: because if it were so, it signifies good in the matter regarding which it is acted upon, if she were joined to malefics (even if she were not joined to benefics); nor does voiding of course harm her in this case as much in those places as much as in others, provided that she is not combust (for then those places[135] do not profit her).

THE 65TH CONSIDERATION is that you look to see whether the Lord of the seventh is impeded or not: because when it is impeded, it signifies the impediment of the quaesited matter, whence it is necessary for you then to defer the judgment if you ever can, and to consider and to investigate in every way that you can, so that you see whence the impediment could come, first from the conjunction of the Lord of the seventh with the planets, then from its separation from them. Likewise from the Moon, because it hardly ever happens but

---

[128] Presumably, impeded by being void in course.

[129] Reading *annora* (with Tr. 7, Part 2, 6th House, Ch. 12) for *ancra*.

[130] From Gr. *psilôthron*, a depilatory instrument.

[131] An interesting example of linguistic elitism: Bonatti describes the Greek-derived *psilotrum* as the true Latin word, while condemning the truly Latinate *sconapotum* as something merely common or vulgar (*vulgariter*). Note that in Tr. 7, Part 2, 6th House, Ch. 12, Bonatti gives the name as *sconapilos*, the more likely Latinate word (as *pilus* means "hair").

[132] See Tr. 7, Part 2, 6th House, Ch. 12 for bathing; Tr. 6, Part 2, 12th House, Ch. 6 for feasts.

[133] *Super radios.*

[134] *Super radios.*

[135] *Loca.*

that you will find the cause of the impediment whence [the cause] would come; for you could judge safely after that.

THE 66TH CONSIDERATION is that you look to see, in questions, and in all things which you intend to do, when the malefic planets threaten some evil, if the place into which their threats fall were the dignity of some benefic; and see if the benefic then were to aspect that place by a trine or sextile aspect: because it will take away all the evil, and it will be wholly annihilated. If indeed it were to aspect from a square aspect, it will take away from the evil, and decrease it, even though it would not destroy it entirely (it might decrease it by half, or a little less). If indeed it were to aspect from the opposition, it will take away from it again, perhaps one-fourth less, or a fifth, or a sixth, or at least one-eighth. If however it did not aspect, the evil will come in accordance with what that impeding malefic had threatened; and it will come from good and just men who do not act by evil means; and perhaps it will happen because the just men will give testimony against him who asks by telling the truth against him, for which reason he will suffer harm or detriment; or perhaps by a judge or ruler who will judge against him for reasons of justice.

If however the place were the dignity of some malefic, the evil will come from unjust men, and those do not employ justice, or truth, but are wicked men, who perhaps carry out testimony against the truth, whether the testimony is true or false: it will be of the sort I have said. Or it will come to him from a bad authority or judge, and a wicked man; even though he will judge justly in the matter (but there will be however much there is in him);[136] nor will it be a man who loves, or fears, or cares about, God.

THE 67TH CONSIDERATION is that you look to see, in questions or in any beginnings, whether there will be an eclipse near the question or the beginning, which is distant from the significator of the matter (or the Moon) by less than 12°: because the eclipse will bring harm and evil to the querent, and to the matter which ought to have been begun, unless a benefic were there who had dignity in that place (because then the malice is decreased). Nevertheless it is necessary for you to look, if there were not a benefic there, to see which one aspects the place of the eclipse (and in what way). Because if the benefics were to aspect, the evil will be increased; if indeed the malefics were to aspect, it will be decreased–which will seem as though something miraculous.

THE 68TH CONSIDERATION is that you look to see, in questions about sick people or at the beginnings of illnesses, whether or not the Lord of the seventh

---

[136] *Tamen erit talis quantum est in se.*

[sign] is free, and the seventh [sign] itself, from impediments. Because if it were free from the malefics, so that it is not impeded by any of them, then the sick person could commit himself confidently to the care of doctors; for the medical arts will be useful to him. If for instance the 7th and its Lord were impeded, Ptolemy said that then the doctor should be removed from the sick person;[137] for the medical arts will not be useful to him, nor the care of the doctors; because the seventh [sign] signifies the medical art, as Sahl says;[138] or perhaps the illness will be made chronic. You can say the same if the aforesaid impediment were at the hour of the beginning of the [medical] care of some illness.[139]

THE 69TH CONSIDERATION is that you look to see, in questions about journeys or in their beginnings, or even in other matters, whether the significators of the Ascendant and the house signifying the quaesited matter (or the undertaking, or the thing to be begun) are equal in strength or weakness: because you could not judge confidently then. For then it will be necessary for you to see the Lord of the conjunction or prevention (insofar as the matter is conjunctional or preventional) which was before the matter about which you intend to act, and you will judge according to it.[140]

Which if again the Lord of the conjunction or the prevention and the Lord of the quaesited matter were equal [in strength], you could not judge with confidence: you would return then to the Moon and see to whom she were originally joined, and you could judge according to that; which if she were not joined to any in the sign or from the sign in which she was, you will change her from the sign in which she is, and see to whom she first is joined in the sign or from the sign in which she were to enter after her exit from the one in which

---

137 *Cent.*, Aph. 57.

138 This is not so: Sahl says "For the Ascendant signifies the doctor; and the Midheaven signifies the sick person; and the seventh sign signifies the infirmity; indeed the fourth sign signifies the medicine" (*On Quest.*, 6th House, "If an infirm person will get better or die"). In Sahl's scheme, the doctor is the active person (Ascendant) battling the infirmity (seventh sign), and the patient (Midheaven) is confronted by the medicine (fourth sign). Moreover, by being in the tenth sign from the doctor, the patient is the focus of the doctor's action. But Sahl does say that if the seventh sign is afflicted, the patient will go from illness to illness. This may simply be a misprint or clerical error on a typesetter's part, as Bonatti correctly gives Sahl's scheme in Tr. 6, Part 2, 6th House, Ch. 1.

139 In other words, we can cast a medical chart not only for the moment of the decumbiture (when the patient takes to bed), but also when the treatment begins. See Tr. 6, Part 2, 6th House.

140 Bonatti seems to be referring to horaries about future actions, and electional charts for the time of the action itself. So if it were a question about something taking place next week, and tomorrow is a New Moon, we would look at the Lord of tomorrow's syzygy, not that of the syzygy preceding the time of the question. Likewise, when electing a time for action, one would look at the syzygy preceding the times one is deciding between.

she was at the time of the named question or beginning–and you will judge according to that. And this is such a heading [or topic] that it is necessary that you consider it well.

THE 70ᵀᴴ CONSIDERATION is that you look at another certain hidden thing, namely one which is not well investigated by astrologers, and sometimes–or rather often–it harms them much: and this is that you see in questions or the beginnings of things whether the Lord of the conjunction of prevention which was before the question, or before the beginning, is in one of the angles of the quaesited matter or undertaking.[141] Because it will then signify that the matter will be perfected, and will come to be–unless it were to remain still because of the querent or inceptor ([or] unless God stops it)–even if it does not seem through the other significators that it ought to be perfected. Which if it were not so, but it were in the succeedents, and the other significators (namely the Lord of the Ascendant and the Lord of the quaesited, and likewise the Moon, or one of them) were to help, the matter will come to be with ease; and if it were in the cadents, it will hardly ever come to be, even if the other significators seem to be favorable; which if they were not favorable, or at least two of them, it will never be perfected.

THE 71ˢᵀ CONSIDERATION is that you look to see, in a question which was made for you about some matter (or if you wished to make some beginning), whether it were a journey or something else, whether the significator fell between the Ascendant and the 12ᵗʰ: because then it will signify a time of lastingness when the matter ought to come to be; and if it were made, how much it ought to last, and they will be days or hours. If however it were between the 12ᵗʰ and the 10ᵗʰ, it will signify half-weeks. If indeed it were between the 10ᵗʰ and the 7ᵗʰ, it will signify months or weeks. If however it were between the 7ᵗʰ and the 4ᵗʰ, it will signify years. And if it were between the 4ᵗʰ and the Ascendant, it will signify half-years.

THE 72ᴺᴰ CONSIDERATION is that you look to see whether a question is about a journey (or if it is the beginning of some journey), and if the Moon were then impeded: because then the journey is not to be made. If indeed it could not come to be but that the journey will happen, put the one who impeded the Moon [as] the Lord of the Ascendant.

THE 73ᴿᴰ CONSIDERATION is that you look to see in questions whether the question signifies good or evil; and see if it signified good, and the benefics were

---

[141] Does this mean "in one of the angles of the chart," or "in one of the angles, counting the quaesited matter as the 1ˢᵗ house/sign?"

to aspect the significator of the question or the Moon: because then the good will be increased. If however the malefics were to aspect, it will be decreased. If indeed it were to signify evil, and the benefics were to aspect, evil will be decreased. If however the malefics were to aspect the significator or the Moon, the evil will be increased and it will come out worse.

THE 74TH CONSIDERATION is that you look to see whether a planetary significator is in its first station, wanting to retrograde: because then it signifies disobedience, and that the matter about which the question was, will not come to be nor be perfected, even if it seems it ought to be perfected. And if it were then some work undertaken, or a building, it will not be completed. And if such a significator, so disposed, were then below the earth, the building will not be erected; which [if] it is said to be erected up to 30 years, still it will not be completed then. And if it were then erected a little bit, it will be erected up to another 30 years. And if it were not completed then, it will not be completed up to 90 years from the day of its first beginning; which if it were not completed then, it will not be completed forever, unless perhaps its ownership were transferred to strangers, and not the usual owners.[142]

And[143] when it is in its second station, wanting to go direct, it signifies that the matter will be perfected, however with delay and complications and duress, and difficulty and effort, and great worry. And if some building were then begun, it will be completed, even if not as quickly as will be believed at the start, provided that the significator is not below the earth–because then he who begins the building will not perfect it, nor even erect it far above the ground. And may you understand this: because a planet in its second station, when it wishes to go direct, signifies the fitness and renewal, and the [forward] direction, and strength of any matter. But in the first [station], when it wants to go retrograde, it signifies dissolution and difficulty, and the destruction of any matter. Understand all of this well, because it will come before your hands most often.

THE 75TH CONSIDERATION is that you look to see whether the Moon, in some matter which someone intends to do, is impeded by one of the planets, of whatever sort the question was, or whatever the beginning was: because then whatever was done or undertaken, will be impeded. However, if the Moon were in a good place from the Ascendant, so that she aspects it by a praiseworthy

---

[142] Bonatti does not address this question in Tr. 6. The question must be, "will this building be finished?"

[143] This paragraph is Bonatti's own, not Lilly's (as Coley's edition reads).

aspect (namely by trine or sextile), and he who were to impede the Moon were to aspect the Ascendant by one of the aforesaid aspects, the impediment will be decreased, nor will it harm so much; and perhaps it will disappear entirely insofar as the one impeding were well disposed–so that it is not cadent from the angles, nor from the Ascendant, as I said, nor were it in its fall (namely in the seventh from its own domicile). For then it will introduce fear more than it brings in harm.

Indeed Sahl seems to want to say that if the impeding malefic were cadent from the Ascendant, or were retrograde, it then introduces fear on the part of the querent or the one making the beginning.[144] I however remember [that] I always feared[145] the impediment of the Moon more than the other impediments, nor do I remember having seen a good end to any matter in which the Moon was impeded: because in journeys, if the journey were to war, I feared for the person of the one journeying to it. If however it were to a business deal, or to another similar thing, I feared distress and anger, and sorrow in the journey, with the loss of substance.

THE 76TH CONSIDERATION is that you look to see from which of the planets the Moon were being separated, and to whom she is joined: because he from whom she is being separated, signifies that which has already been. Indeed he to whom she is joined, signifies that which is going to be, as is said elsewhere. Which if she were being separated from a malefic, and is joined to a benefic, it signifies that that which already was, was not good, but rather was an evil thing, and something impeding the querent; and that which is going to be, will be good, and something about which the querent will rejoice, and will be useful to him. While if she were being separated from a benefic, and were joined to a malefic, the matter was good from the beginning, but the end will be evil. If for example she was being separated from a benefic and was joined to a benefic, the matter was good, and is good, and its end is to be praised. If indeed she were being separated from a malefic and is joined to another malefic, the matter was evil, and is evil, and its end will be evil.

THE 77TH CONSIDERATION is that you look to see whether the Lord of the Ascendant of some question, or of any other matter, or the Moon, were in the opposition of its own domicile–that is, the Moon in Capricorn, Mercury in Sagittarius or Pisces, Venus in Scorpio or Aries, the Sun in Aquarius, Mars in

---

144 Judgment 4, but Sahl does not mention retrogradation there.
145 This statement is a suggestion that Bonatti had retired from active practice by the time he wrote this Treatise.

Taurus or Libra, Jupiter in Gemini or Virgo, Saturn in Cancer or Leo. Because then the Lord of the question or of whatever other matter, will be inappropriate for [or averse to] the purpose for which he asks, or concerning which it is done; nor will it be a matter in which he will delight, or which he strives to make perfected. And it will seem more likely that he does not want it to be perfected, than that he does want it to be perfected or to come to be.

THE 78TH CONSIDERATION is that you look at the sign which signifies the matter about which the question was. For the 1st signifies the person.[146] The 2nd signifies substance. The 3rd signifies brothers, the 4th signifies parents, *etc.*, as was said above in the Treatise on the twelve houses. And you would see its house, and according to what it showed you about the matter which it signified, [and] according to the thing to be judged you could estimate everything and the individual things[147] which I told you, they having been diligently inspected.

THE 79TH CONSIDERATION is that you look to see whether a planetary significator or the Moon is joined to benefic or malefic planets, whether by conjunction or by aspect. And you must inquire into this diligently, because the corporal conjunction of the Sun is the greatest misfortune which can befall the planets.

THE 80TH CONSIDERATION is that you look to see in which sign the significator of the quaesited matter is from its own domicile—whether in the same one, or in the second or in the third or in the fourth or in the fifth or in the sixth or in the seventh or the eighth or in the ninth or in the tenth or in the eleventh or the twelfth. Because according to what is signified by that sign in which it was from its own domicile, according to that you will judge just as you judged about any of the planets located in one of the houses from the Ascendant.[148]

THE 81ST CONSIDERATION is that you look to see whether a planetary significator is in an angle or in a succeedent, or in a cadent, because however much the significator were closer to the line of the angle, by that much more it will be stronger. And however much it were farther from it, by that much more it will be less strong; and so on in a succeedent. And however much it were closer to the line of a house cadent from the angle, by that much more will it be weak. And however much it were farther from it, by that much more will it be weaker.

THE 82ND CONSIDERATION is that you look to see whether the planetary significator of some matter accepts the disposition of one of the planets,

---

[146] By "person" Bonatti means the physical body itself.

[147] *Secundum illud iudicandum esse poteris aestimare, omnibus & singulis.*

[148] In other words, we may work with derived whole sign houses from the domicile of the significator.

whether benefic or malefic. Because if it were to receive disposition from a benefic, it signifies good; and better than that if the benefic were of good condition, and well disposed. If however it were not well disposed, it will be less than this. Indeed if it were impeded, it will be less again than this. If by chance it were to receive the disposition from a malefic, it signifies the contrary; and more strongly so if the malefic were impeded. If however it were not impeded, it will be somewhat less than this. If by chance it were well disposed, it will be decreased more again from its malice.

THE 83RD CONSIDERATION is that you look to see whether the benefics and malefics are equal [in strength] in a question or any other matter. Because then they will not signify[149] any conclusive judgment (namely good or evil), nor will the matter about which it is done, bring in wealth nor harm.

THE 84TH CONSIDERATION is that you look to see if the benefics were stronger than the malefics in questions: because if both were strong, and the benefics prevailed in strength, they will signify something good as though middling; if indeed the malefics prevailed, they will signify something evil as though middling.

THE 85TH CONSIDERATION is that you look to see whether the Part of Fortune falls in a good place in the figure or in a bad angle (namely in a succeedent or in a cadent [respectively]). And see how it is aspected, and by whom, whether by a benefic or by a malefic, and whether or not it is received by him by whom it is aspected. Because sometimes questions seem good, and the Part of Fortune falls in a bad place, which weakens a question much and makes it less useful: for the querent will hope for a good thing and it will not come to him as the question seems to show. For the good which the question seemed to signify will be reduced on account of the Part of Fortune being located in a bad place in the figure or joined to a malefic planet. And sometimes a question will seem to threaten evil, and to pronounce it; however, if the Part of Fortune were in a good place in the figure, and were joined to a benefic planet (who received it) by body or by aspect, the evil will be reduced, and not so much of what the question seems to threaten, will happen to the querent.

THE 86TH CONSIDERATION is that you look to see in every question, or journey, or nativity, or any other beginning, whether one of the malefics aspects the significator; and see if both were retrograde, and cadent, and peregrine, and in signs totally contrary to their nature: then they will bring in such contrariety, and such harm, that it could never be escaped, nor could anyone avoid it, unless

---

[149] Reading *significabunt* for *significabuntur*.

God alone made it [so]. And it will be practically a great miracle if he whom the danger threatened, escaped it. And if someone were born with the matter appearing this way, he will be a beggar and pauper his whole life, and needing food in his belly, and he will never be able to exert himself so that he could escape his beggary. And if it were then a house that was built, one will never rejoice in it, nor collect money on it which could profit him; and contrary things will often happen to him by which his goods[150] will be erased and disappear, and will come to nothing. And always when he believes some business of his to be going better, and to be coming afterwards to a good and desired end, then it will more likely be destroyed and frustrated, unless divine goodness interposes itself.

THE 87TH CONSIDERATION is that you look at the ninth-part[151] of the Moon, which is something very much to be observed: because it often impedes the astrologer so that he cannot well observe the truth, and sometimes he errs in judging, not knowing the reason that causes him to err.

THE 88TH CONSIDERATION is that you consider the planet from which the Moon is being separated [and] how it is disposed, because it signifies what already was, as was said above. And see to whom she is now joined, so that there is not a distance of more than 5' between them: because it signifies what presently is, according to how it is disposed. Even see whose conjunction she seeks, or to whom she will first be joined after her separation from him to whom she is now joined: because he will signify what is going to be in the matter according to how he is disposed.

THE 89TH CONSIDERATION is that you look at the twelfth-parts[152] of the Moon, which is even a thing very much to be observed in many judgments, even more than the aforesaid [ninth-parts],[153] because greater dangers could supervene from [both] it and from the most subtle and uncommon considerations of the astrologers, which is poorly observed by many and often (on account of laziness more than on account of ignorance): whence they sometimes fall into disgrace among laymen on account of the fear of labor which they do not want to keep up.

---

150 Reading *bona* for *bono*.

151 *Novenarium*. These are defined in Tr. 9, Part 3, 12th House, Ch. 12.

152 Reading *duodecimae* for *duodenaria*. This refers to the twelve 2° 30' divisions of each sign, each one allotted to each of the other signs, not to the *duodena* (the hours of the lunar month attributed to various triplicity rulers), especially given that they are mentioned right after the ninth-parts (87th Consideration).

153 Compare with Coley, who only says "even more than divers things that we have said" (p. 38).

THE 90TH CONSIDERATION is that you look to see, in questions or nativities, or journeys, or any other matters or beginnings, whether the Lord of the domicile in which the Sun was, and the Lord of the domicile in which the Moon was, and the Lord of the Ascendant–are oriental, and in angles (even though this rarely happens), and they aspect each other from good places, and from good and praiseworthy aspects (namely by trines or sextiles): because then they signify the greatest fortune, and the greatest good, and the ultimate progress in every matter, of whatever sort it is. If indeed they were not all so disposed, but [only] some of them, it will signify good according to that portion which were so disposed.

THE 91ST CONSIDERATION is that you look to see in questions, or nativities, or in other matters of whatever sort they were, whether Mars is in one of the angles of the figure, especially if the angles were fixed signs: and particularly if Scorpio were the 1st house: because then Mars destroys all good which is signified by the question or by the figure. And if he does not wholly destroy, he impedes much, and diminishes it–unless perhaps Jupiter then aspected Mars from a trine or sextile aspect, because then the malice of Mars is decreased, and mitigated on account of the aspect of Jupiter–according, however, to how Jupiter were disposed in his strength or weakness.

THE 92ND CONSIDERATION is that you look in nativities, or in universal questions,[154] or in questions about death, and see if the Lord of the house of death, or the significator of death, or the Lord of the house in which the Lord of the house of death was, were to go toward the significator of the native or the querent, or he to him: because that planet so disposed is made the killer, and kills whether he is a benefic or is a malefic, whether or not reception intervenes.

THE 93RD CONSIDERATION is that you look to see, if the question were about a matter which someone wants to seek from another, or were a thing he wanted to dig up or take out of a hidden or secret place, whether the significator of the querent or of the quaesited matter aspects Saturn or is joined to him by body, or if Saturn is in the house [domicile?] of the quaesited matter: because then what the querent seeks will hardly come to be, and the hidden thing will be taken out of the place in which it is with difficulty, and with the greatest labor, and complication, and with delay, even if it seemed that the matter about which it is asked ought to come to be quickly and with ease. And often after the querent

---

[154] These are questions posed about matters without specifying a given time frame or situation: e.g., "Will I be rich?" as opposed to "Will I win this lottery?" See Tr. 6.

has thought the matter to be arranged, it will be impeded and delayed more than he himself believed.

THE 94TH CONSIDERATION is that you look to see in questions or in other beginnings, whether the significator of the quaesited matter is cadent from the Ascendant, or from the other angles, or from the house [domicile?] of the quaesited matter, or from its Lord,[155] or is retrograde or in a bad condition with the Sun, or there is, in the house [domicile?] of the quaesited matter a planet [that is] cadent, or retrograde,[156] or in a bad condition with the Sun, or in a bad place from him, or in a bad disposition with him: because these things signify the impediment of the matter, even if the question otherwise appears to be good.

THE 95TH CONSIDERATION is that you consider whether the planets signifying the quaesited matter are joined to one another: because that signifies the perfection of the matter itself. However, do not judge that the matter is going to perfect in a settled way, unless you look and consider well the nature of the sign in which they are joined (whether it is of their nature): because if it were of their nature, the matter will be perfected with ease, and the joy of the querent. If indeed the planets did not agree in nature with the sign, the matter will not be perfected with ease, but rather hardly or never. And if it were perfected, this will be with the labor and greatest worry of the querent, even if it seemed otherwise like it ought to be perfected easily. And if they did agree, the matter will come to be with little labor, however not very easily.

THE 96TH CONSIDERATION is that you look, in questions which seem to show that the matters about which questions come to be, ought to be perfected, to see whether the significator of the matter and the Moon are in angles, and are both removed from the cusps of the angles by more than 25°. Because this signifies that the matter will not be perfected, even if it seems to be arranged. If indeed only one of them (namely the Lord signifying the quaesited matter, or the Moon) were removed from the angle as was said, and the other was not removed, the matter will be perfected even though with difficulty, unless perhaps it was a journey: because nevertheless it will be perfected, even if the significators were removed from the angles.

THE 97TH CONSIDERATION is that you consider in what clime you take up the question: because judgments are made diverse according to how the ascensions

---

[155] That the planet could be cadent from the Lord suggests that Bonatti may be referring to whole sign houses here.
[156] Reading *retrogradus* for *retrogradui*.

of the climes and regions are made diverse.[157] For there is not the same order in ascensions or elevations of signs in one clime as there is in another; nor is the Ascendant the same in one region as it is in another. Whence unless you watch yourself well, you could err in your judgment, which would be bad, and improper, and very reprehensible. For the signs are raised up one way in the first clime, another way in the second, and another way in the third, and another way in the fourth, another way in the fifth, another way in the sixth, and another way in the seventh.

And[158] therefore it is necessary that you watch out well for these differences, lest you fall into error in your judgments. Because in any direction you were to go from one region to another, whether it were from the east to the west, or from the west into the east, or from the south into the north, or from the north into the south, by 53 *miliaria*,[159] and a certain [amount] hardly perceptible.[160] one Ascendant will be made divergent from another by 1°, from the east to the west according to longitude (and in the opposite direction), and from the south to the north (and in the other direction), and a certain [amount] hardly more, but still perceptible. But perhaps some fools in tunics could rise up and say that "If the judgments are made diverse according to the location of the region, therefore they are false"–not knowing what lies hidden.[161] Nor is anything to be said back to them, nor any debate to be had with them, for they have no discernment, nor do they understand, nor believe, and nothing is acceptable to them.

However there are among them certain discerning people, and those well understanding intelligible things, and you can engage with them (even though they are few)–of which one was the venerable Brother Conradus Brixiensis of the Order of Preachers,[162] whom I found very discerning, and to understand every truth very well, and operating by it, who, on account of his profound wisdom was made the bishop of Cesenas. For these things which I tell you can make the astrologer err, and I fear they have made some people err sometimes; because a judgment cannot be given except according to the Ascendant and the

---

[157] By "clime," Bonatti means sections of geographical latitude; "region" means geographical longitude.

[158] This passage is Bonatti's own, not Lilly's (as Coley's edition makes it seem).

[159] A *miliarium* is a distanced measured by 1,000 units, often paces. An English cognate is "mile," but it is not clear to me that Bonatti meant something close to the modern mile.

[160] See Tr. 8, Part 1, Ch. 5.

[161] *Quid lateret.* I believe Bonatti is saying they do not understand because these matters are obscure to them.

[162] I.e., of the Benedictines.

other houses; whence if the Ascendants are diversified, it must by necessity [be] that the judgments will be diversified. And thus it is necessary that you do not fear labor, nor that laziness conquer your concern, but that you make it so that you own tables of the elevations [ascensions] of the signs for every clime in which you are, and for every region, [whether] made by you or another by [exact] reckoning or by such inference from one region to another so that it does not deceive you.

However, it is more difficult to find the difference from clime to clime than from region to region (and this is according to longitude). Because if you were to have tables of the elevations of the signs in some region from the east to the west, you could make an inference and have the elevations of the signs from that region to another one in which direction you wanted [to go], whether toward the east, or toward the west from it, according to that clime, by taking the diversity just as I told you; but according to the diverse climes you could not so easily make an inference.[163]

THE 98TH CONSIDERATION is that you look to see in questions, if that [matter] which is signified by some question [that it] ought to come to be, is signified by the planets through corporal conjunction, or through an aspect, or through the transfer of light. Because if the significators were conjoined by body or by aspect, the matter will come to be and be perfected by the querent and by the quaesited without the mediation of another. If indeed they were not coinjoined by body or by aspect, but one of the planets were to transfer light between them, the matter will come to be through the agency of legates, or of some person, or of some people who interject themselves into it, and lead the matter to its effect through a person or thing signified by the house [domicile?] whose Lord was the mediator. For if it were the Lord of the 2nd house who transferred the light, the matter will come to be through spending [or expenses], or by the introduction of the querent's money in some other way. If it were the Lord of the 3rd, it will come to be through the querent's brothers (if he had brothers) or by one of those things which are signified by the 3rd house. If it were the Lord of the 4th, it will come to be through the father or through one of those things which are signified by the 4th house. If it were the Lord of the 5th, it will come to be through a child or through one of those things which are signified by the 5th

---

[163] In other words, it is easier to understand how the degree of the Midheaven changes with changes in geographical longitude, than it is to calculate the oblique ascensions and zodiacal longitude of the Ascendant when moving from clime to clime. This is apparent from looking at tables of houses, where the same local sidereal time gives the same Midheaven for many different latitudes.

house. If it were the Lord of the 6th, it will come to be through slaves or through one of those things which are signified by the 6th house. If it were the Lord of the 7th, it will come to be through the wife or through one of those things which are signified by the 7th house. If it were the Lord of the 8th, it will come to be through death, or through the wife's money, or through one of the things which are signified by the 8th house. If it were the Lord of the 9th, it will come to be through some bishop or religious person or through one of those things which are signified by the 9th house. If it were the Lord of the 10th, it will come to be through the king or an authority or through one of those things which are signified by the 10th house. If it were the Lord of the 11th, it will come to be through some friend or through one of those things which are signified through the 11th house. If it were the Lord of the 12th, it will come to be through some hidden enemy or through one of those things which are signified by the 12th house.

THE 99TH CONSIDERATION is that you look to see, in questions or nativities, or in other beginnings, what is going to be from them: because sometimes through a question it will seem that some matter ought to come to be, and to be wholly perfected–[but] it will not be perfected wholly, but in part, and sometimes it will be perfected as a whole, and sometimes not as a whole, nor will it be perfected in part, and why does this happen? Whence astrologers are blamed and blasphemed due to this, and they do not know how to explain themselves, being ignorant of the reason why it happens; and this is a hard and difficult and most delicate investigation; and it was the reason why our ancient [forebears] did not get themselves involved in it, because it would be a very great labor– except for our most honored predecessor Abū Ma'shar (who is to be imitated in all things), [who] said more on this than the other astrologers had said. And I found his judgments, both the particular ones and those concerning revolutions, more effective than the others, and more to be striven after, even if Ptolemy (who was an elucidator of this science) was found more to be emulated in universal judgments than the rest of the astrologers.[164] And it is this (the consideration of certain fixed stars which are in certain signs), which I spoke [about], of which I will make mention to you in the Treatise on revolutions and in the Treatise on nativities, [and] I will touch somewhat on them.

---

[164] By "universal" judgments, Bonatti means general delineations about topics–concerning which Ptolemy used almost exclusively universal or natural significators. Bonatti is praising Abū Ma'shar's ability to predict accurately and precisely.

Nevertheless however, I will name those here which pass through your hands more, and lest you perhaps put off having knowledge of them too long: of which certain ones are of the nature of benefics, or of the nature of the good planets (and those of the nature of benefics perfect matters which do not seem ought to be perfected by the significations of the planets); certain ones are of the nature of malefics, and they are those which do not permit matters to be perfected through what is signified by the planets—of which, of those which are of the nature of the malefics, certain ones are found in every sign.

Of which two are in the head of Aries, namely in the thirteenth degree and the forty-fifth minute; the other is in the fourteenth degree and the forty-fifth minute. And they are of the nature of Saturn and Mars.

In Taurus are six stars in the ninth degree and fifth-fifth minute, which are called the Pleiades (all however are called as one), and they are all of the nature of Mars and the Moon. And another is in its thirteenth degree. And another is in the thirteenth degree and second minute. And another is in the fourteenth degree and forty-fifth minute, and it is called the Devil.[165] And another is in its fifteenth degree, which is called the Head of the Devil.[166] And another is in the belly of Taurus, in the nineteenth degree and fifteenth minute, which is called Aldebaran,[167] all of which are of the nature of Mars and Mercury.

In Gemini is one in its eighth degree, which is called the Shoulder of the Dog,[168] which is of the nature of Mars and Saturn. And another is in its tenth degree and fifteenth minute, which is of the nature of Mars, and is called Bellatrix. Another is in its seventeenth degree and fifty-fifth minute. Another is in its eighteenth degree and fifty-second minute, which is called the Witch,[169] and is of the nature of the Sun and Mars.

Another is in Cancer in its second degree and third minute, which is called the Camel, and is of the nature of Saturn and the Moon. And another is in its seventh degree and fifty-fifth minute. And another is in its

---

[165] *Diabolus.*
[166] *Caput diaboli,* i.e. Algol.
[167] *Aldeboran.*
[168] *Humerus canis.*
[169] *Malefica,* lit. "Evildoer" (fem.).

thirteenth degree, and is of the nature of the Sun and the Moon, which is called Killer of the Camel.[170] And another is in the same degree, of the nature of Saturn, which is called the Foot of the Dog.[171] And another is in the seventeenth degree and fifty-fifth minute, both [of which] are of the nature of Saturn.

Indeed in Leo one of them[172] is in its fifteenth degree and fifty-fifth minute, of the nature of Saturn.

In Virgo however are two stars, of which one is in its seventh degree and the eleventh minute, and is of the nature of Mars. And the other is in its fifteenth degree, and it is of the nature of Saturn.

In Libra is one star in the twenty-sixth degree, of the nature of Saturn.

In Scorpio are three stars, of which one is in the first degree and the third minute of it, and the other in the eighth degree and seventh minute, and the other in the ninth degree, all of which are of the nature of Mars.

In Sagittarius are two small stars, of which one is in its nineteenth degree and second minute. The other is in its twenty-first degree and first minute, and they are of the nature of Saturn.

In Capricorn are two stars (which are called evil), of which one is in its twenty-seventh degree and second minute; and the other is in its twenty-ninth degree and fifth minute. Both are of the nature of Saturn.

In Aquarius, one star [is] in its ninth degree and fourth minute, of the nature of Mars and Saturn.

In Pisces for instance, is one star in its fourth degree and seventh minute, of the nature of Mars and Mercury.

---

170 *Occidens camelum.*
171 *Pes canis.*
172 Either Bonatti means "one of the fixed stars," or "one of two," (although he does not provide a second star).

All of the aforesaid stars are harmers and malevolent, and impeders and destroyers of matters after they seem they ought to be perfected, and prohibitors lest they be perfected; whence it is always necessary for you to avoid them in all your actions, if you ever can (which is very difficult). And even though I have made mention of them to you here, you will find this said below (and better) in the Treatise on the revolutions of years, if health and life be granted to me.

THE 100TH CONSIDERATION is that you look in your actions at the fixed stars helping matters so they come to be and are perfected, of which is such a place [for naming them]:

For in Aries are two stars, of which one is in its fifteenth degree and sixth minute, which is of the nature of Jupiter and Venus, whose nature is to aid and advance. Another is in its twenty-sixth degree and first minute, of the nature of Jupiter.

Indeed in Taurus are three stars, of which one is in its first degree and third minute. And another is in the eighth degree and seventh minute of the same [sign]. Another is in its ninth degree and first minute, which are all of the nature of Venus.

However in Gemini are two stars, of which one is in its nineteenth degree and second minute. And another is in its twenty-first degree and third minute, which are of the nature of Jupiter, and are of the second magnitude.

In Cancer are again two stars (which are called good), of which one is in its twenty-seventh degree and second minute. And another is in its twenty-ninth degree and fifth minute, and both are of the nature of Jupiter.

And for instance in Leo is one star in its ninth degree and fourth minute, of the nature of Jupiter and Venus.

Indeed in Virgo is one star in its fourth degree and seventh minute, which is of the nature of Venus and the Moon.

However, in Libra are two stars of the nature of Jupiter and Venus, of which one is in its thirteenth degree and forty-fifth minute, and the other is in its fourteenth degree and forty-fifth minute.

Indeed in Scorpio are four stars, of which one is in its ninth degree and fifty-fifth minute. And another is in the thirteenth degree and first minute. And another is in its fourteenth degree and forty-fifth minute. And the fourth is in its nineteenth degree and fifteenth minute, which are all of the nature of Jupiter.

Indeed in Sagittarius are two stars, of which one is in its tenth degree and fifteenth minute. And the other is [in] its seventh degree and fifty-fifth minute; and both are of the nature of Jupiter.

In Capricorn are three stars, of which one is in its second degree and third minute. And the other is in its seventh degree and fifty-fifth minute. And another is in its seventeenth degree and fifty-fifth minute, which are all of the nature of Jupiter.

And in Aquarius is one star, which is in its fifteenth degree and fifty-fifth minute, of the nature of Jupiter.

Indeed in Pisces are two stars, of which one is in its seventh degree and eleventh minute, and it is of the nature of Venus. And the other is in its fourteenth degree and fifty-ninth minute, and it is of the nature of Jupiter.

Whence always if you were to see the significator of some matter joined corporally with one of the aforesaid helping fixed stars, you will pronounce good, and the increase of the matter, and a good end.

THE 101ST CONSIDERATION is that you look, in nativities or questions, to see which planet is the killer or cutter[173] of life or years, or the prohibitor of the matter so that it does not come to be or be perfected: because that one is he who destroys the life of the native and kills, and prohibits matters so they do not come to be, and destroys them, who is stronger by a multitude of dignities

---

[173] *Abscisor*, the "abscisor." See Tr. 6, Part 2, Ch. 5.

or powers in the nativity or question, or at the beginning of some matter.[174] However, Māshā'allāh hid this, and it seems as though he did it well, because he revealed it (and a certain other, very useful secret) to a certain student of his alone, who, led by arrogance, appropriated it for himself.[175]

Indeed after you were to perceive the one who was the prohibitor or destroyer, or killer, see to whom the Lord of the Ascendant or the Moon (who is the participator in every matter) is joined, just as was said to you elsewhere, or the Lord of whichever quaesited matter or undertaking, or beginning, and the Lord of the domicile of the Moon, namely one of them or more of them: because if it is joined to a retrograde or combust planet, or one cadent from the Ascendant or from an angle, or to one of the malefics who did not receive him, or to another unfortunate star which is made unfortunate by the malefics who cut off[176] the light of the significator, the matter is destroyed, and is not perfected, and thus the years of the native are cut off and are diminished, and he will not live a long time. Besides [that] if the Lord of the Ascendant, or the Moon, or the Lord of the quaesited matter is joined to a planet who is free from the conjunction of the malefics, and is sound as much as [he is] in himself, but is joined to another planet impeded by one of the aforesaid impediments—the matter will be destroyed even after it will seem and be believed to be arranged so that it ought to be perfected; and the life of the native will be cut off when it seems (and is well believed that) he ought to live. And this will happen even if it is not a conjunction with the cutter, provided that the significator or the Moon is impeded just as was said, by one of the aforesaid impediments.

THE 102ND CONSIDERATION is that you look and see in matters which are signified, what kind of signification that is signified ought to be found, and from what significators it ought to be extracted. For it is extracted from the significator of the querent, and from the significator of the quaesited matter itself. Whence if the significator of the querent and the significator of the quaesited matter were joined, and likewise the Moon, it signifies the complete effecting of the matter; if indeed [they] were not joined, it signifies the contrary.[177]

---

[174] This does not quite seem right, since one would normally think this planet would be best placed to perfect a matter. Perhaps something is missing, or in an as-yet untranslated text there is reference to Māshā'allāh on this matter (see next sentence).

[175] I do not know what Bonatti is referring to.

[176] Reading *abscindunt* for *abscindit*.

[177] Having all three planets joined is an ideal condition Bonatti does not always insist on. See Tr. 6, Part 1.

And from the conjunction of the significators ought to be known why the question arose; and through the Lord of the house [domicile?] in which the conjunction comes to be, ought to be known what the question will be about: for if it were a benefic, it will be about something good according to the nature [or condition][178] of, and what is signified by, that benefic, and the house in which it is, and [according to] what is signified by the Lord of that house, and by the place in which the Lord of the house is, even in which [the benefic] is. If however if were a malefic, it signifies that it will be about something bad according to the nature [or condition][179] of, and what is signified by, that malefic, and the house in which it is, and [according to] what is signified by the Lord of that house, and by the place in which the Lord of the house is, even in which [the malefic] is. Which if the Lord of the domicile (or the Lord of the exaltation, or the Lord of the other two lesser dignities) were to aspect, or a transfer of light were to come to be, the reason why the question arose will be known. If indeed it were not [known] by one of these, it will not be known determinately why the question arose, but it will be for a reason which is not yet known; and from the aspect of the benefics or malefics will be known of what sort the effecting of the matter will be.

THE 103ᴿᴰ CONSIDERATION is that you look to see, in nativities or universal questions, in which house the Part of Fortune were found. Because from what is signified by that house, will be the fortune or wealth of the native or the querent, if it were well-disposed. If however it were poorly disposed, it signifies that for that reason there will be misfortune and harm.

THE 104ᵀᴴ CONSIDERATION is that you look to see, in nativities or in universal questions, or of whatever other thing, whether the significator of the native or the querent is found in the 7th from its own domicile, or in opposition to the Lord of the Ascendant:[180] because it will not signify wealth for him from what is signified by that house, but rather harm and expenses.

THE 105ᵀᴴ CONSIDERATION is that you look to see in nativities or in universal questions, whether a malefic that is made unfortunate is found in the seventh, because it signifies that the native or querent will not rejoice with his wives, nor with girlfriends, nor with his partners, but he will always have arguments and bad will with them; rarely will it happen to him otherwise from this [area of life].

---

[178] *Esse.*

[179] *Esse.*

[180] Since the significator of a native is (and that of the querent usually is) the Lord of the Ascendant, I am not sure what Bonatti is getting at here.

THE 106TH CONSIDERATION is that you look to see, in nativities or in universal questions, or in any matters, if a benefic that is made fortunate, not impeded, were in the seventh: because it signifies that the native or querent will be fortunate in having good wives and good partners; but nevertheless he will have many rivals, and many who hate him, with reason and without reason, and more likely out of envy than for something his fault, so that he will hardly be able to perfect what he wants, and he will perfect it together with labor and obstacles.

THE 107TH CONSIDERATION is that you look to see, in nativities or universal questions, or other ones, whether Mars is in the second from the Ascendant, or in the tenth, and well-disposed: for it signifies that the native or querent will have fortune in those things which operate by iron, or fire, or consuming, as are workshops, furnaces, and the like; taverns, inns, and the like. If however it were a malefic and badly disposed, you could judge the contrary.

THE 108TH CONSIDERATION is that you look to see if one of the planets were to aspect two domiciles:[181] because its strength will be in that in which it were to have the greater dignity, and more strengths, and it will be more helped by it and by what it signifies.

THE 109TH CONSIDERATION is that you look to see, in nativities or in universal questions, if the Lord of the 5th house [domicile?] were in the seventh, impeded; because it signifies that the native will not be fortunate in banquets [or entertainments], and many disagreeable things will happen to him at them, and worse and more detestable dishes will be served to him than to the other reclining [guests]–and fouler desserts, and worse gifts [or wreaths],[182] and perhaps that gifts [or wreaths] will not be given to him, unless he first seeks them out, even if they are hardly given to all the others. And if something is taken away from the table, it is more likely to be taken from him than from one of the others. The same thing will happen to him with respect to clothing and other bodily ornaments.

THE 110TH CONSIDERATION is that you look to see in nativities and in universal questions, whether the Ascendant is Scorpio: because he whose Ascendant it was, will not have fortune [good luck] in the Roman Church, on account of Cancer, the exaltation of Jupiter, who naturally signifies clerics, which will then be the 9th house [domicile?], which signifies the Church; and Jupiter is the enemy of Mars, who is the Lord of the Ascendant.

---

[181] *Aspexerit duas domus.* Every planet at every moment aspects multiple domiciles; perhaps Bonatti is simply trying to point out that we can compare them, and there is nothing special about there being two of them.

[182] *Ciphi*, equivalent to Gr. *kiphoi/ stephanoi.*

THE 111TH CONSIDERATION is that you look and see, in nativities and in universal questions, and even in other questions, and especially in [questions of] lawsuits and controversies, whether the Tail of the Dragon is in the seventh: because it signifies detriment and the voiding[183] of the enemies, and the increasing of the native or querent, because then the Head will be in the first. If indeed [the Tail] were in the eighth, it signifies the voiding and decrease of the substance and goods of [the enemies] (and even in the seventh), and the increase of the goods and substance of the native or the querent, because then the Head will be in the second. When it is in the third, it signifies the voiding of the brothers; in the fourth, the voiding of the parents. In the fifth, the voiding of children. In the sixth, the voiding of slaves. In the seventh and eighth, what I told you. In the ninth, the voiding of journeys. In the tenth, the voiding of men. In the eleventh, the voiding of friends. In the twelfth, the voiding of larger animals. And it even signifies in every house [domicile?], the voiding of the other significators of that house. Saturn and Mars do the same thing, but somewhat less so than what the Tail does. And even other malefics[184] empty out the aforesaid signified things, still however somewhat less than what Saturn and Mars do, unless the malefics themselves were the significators (because then it reduces much of their malice).

THE 112TH CONSIDERATION is that you look at the Ascendant in nativities or questions, for [if] Virgo were ascending [in] any one of them, and Mercury were of good condition, or at least he was not made unfortunate, it signifies that if the native or querent were to pursue the medical art, he will be fortunate in being a doctor, and it will go well for him in his medical practice or cures, but he will be unfortunate in his salary and in gaining wealth by the art of medicine, because they to whom he offers his service will be unwilling to recompense him, and he will hardly be able to go after them as he ought to, except for very few of them, and he will be unfortunate in his lawsuits. And if he were to pursue law, he will be unfortunate in his advocacy, and he will be despised by low-quality people, not to mention by others; nor will his words be heard, and even after he speaks useful words and words of wisdom, they will be counted as nothing by those who hear them; for they in whose service he has spoken will hear rather a fool and idiot, even though there are few who know how to improve on his speech. And for the most part, of things he gets involved in, it will be unlucky

---

183 In this Consideration, "voiding" (or "emptying") should be considered in context: i.e., loss of money, no children, *etc.*
184 Bonatti means planets that are naturally benefic, but are malefic because of their condition.

for him, and men will be his enemies for no reason, and will say bad things about him, not knowing how to express why. But it will be otherwise if the Ascendant were Taurus or Pisces, and Jupiter and Venus and Mercury were all together in the Ascendant, [or] Jupiter and Venus in the Sun's *kasmīmī* (of whatever sort the Ascendant was): [for] he is going to be treated like a prophet, and his words considered mellifluous, though he made foolish things public.

THE 113TH CONSIDERATION is that you look to see, in nativities or questions, whether one of the malefics is impeded in the ninth, who did not have dignity there: because it signifies that the native or querent will be accused and found guilty, with cause and without cause. If indeed there were an unimpeded benefic there (and better yet if it were to have dignity there), it signifies that he will be praised and honored with cause and without cause.

THE 114TH CONSIDERATION is that you look to see, in nativities or questions, whether the Lord of the 8th house [domicile?] is a benefic and is in the second: because it signifies that the native or querent will acquire [wealth] and gain wealth from the goods of the dead, and enemies, and wives, and all the more strongly if it were not impeded or had dignity there. If however it were a malefic, it signifies the diminution of the substance of the native or querent, unless perhaps it were to have dignity there. But if it were to have dignity there, and were otherwise well-disposed, and of good condition, it will cause little or no harm. If indeed it did not have dignity there, and were otherwise of bad condition, it signifies the total destruction of the substance, and the loss of it in every way.

THE 115TH CONSIDERATION is that you look to see, in nativities or questions, if the 8th house or its Lord were impeded: because it signifies that the native or querent will be harmed by reason of the death of some women whose dowry he will have to return, with harm to him.

THE 116TH CONSIDERATION is that you look to see, in nativities or questions, which of the houses were impeded or made unfortunate, or its Lord were impeded or made unfortunate: because[185] it signifies that on account of those things which are signified by that house, harm will come to the native or the querent. Indeed whichever [house] were made fortunate (or its Lord), good and usefulness will come to him on account of those things which are signified by that house.

THE 117TH CONSIDERATION is that you look to see, in nativities or questions, in which of them the Tail of the Dragon were in the 4th: because it signifies that

---

[185] Reading *quoniam* for *quonidam*.

whatever the native or the querent were to acquire or earn, will be destroyed, and come to nothing. And in whichever other house it were in, it signifies that harm and detriment will come to the native or querent in these things, and from these things, which are signified by that house.

THE 118TH CONSIDERATION is that you look to see, in nativities or questions, in which house there was a benefic made fortunate and strong, and well-disposed, not impeded: because it signifies that from those people and from those matters which are signified by that house, the native or querent will earn money and have fortune in them. And in whichever one were a malefic, he will lose, and his misfortune will then be from the matters signified by it.

THE 119TH CONSIDERATION is that you look to see, in nativities or questions, if the Lord of the 2nd house were in the 7th, and the 7th were Aries or Scorpio or Capricorn or Aquarius: because it signifies that the enemies of the native or querent readily take away his goods from him. And if he were to have a partnership with someone, he will steal away from him the amount the native or querent put together with him–likewise his wife or girlfriend will steal from him whatever is convenient for her to be able to steal–unless the Lord of the Ascendant is in a trine or sextile aspect with the Lord of the seventh [sign], or in the other aspects with reception.

THE 120TH CONSIDERATION is that you look to see, in nativities or questions, whether some Lord of any of these eight houses–the 3rd, 4th, 5th, 6th, 9th, 10th, 11th, 12th, is in the 7th–because whichever one of them were in it,[186] will be inimical to the native or querent, unless perfect reception intervenes and from a good aspect (namely by a trine or sextile). If however [it were] a square or an opposite,[187] with reception, it will subtract from the malice, however it will not wholly remove it. So if it were the Lord of the 3rd, his brothers will be inimical to him; if it were the Lord of the 4th, his father will be inimical to him; if it were the Lord of the 5th, his children will be inimical to him; if it were the Lord of the 6th, his slaves will be inimical to him; if it were the Lord of the 9th, religious figures will be inimical to him, and will oppose him, and speak evil about him, nor however will he entrust things being perfected[188] to them. If it were the Lord of the 10th, kings, nobles, the wealthy and the powerful will be inimical to him, nor will he make money with them or by a favorable opportunity with them; indeed he will lose just as much from another party, or more (however it

---

[186] Reading *ea* for *eo*.

[187] *Oppositus.*

[188] *Perfica.* That is, matters that need to get done.

will be worse for him with the powerful). And, however, even if at some time one or more seem favorable to him, still an evil will be shown to him by some one of the others, or perhaps by many, so that if others bequeath him something in a letter, they will recover it from him in time. And perhaps that one of the powerful will expel him from the city on account of the offenses he will commit by taking a part in the household or place at the table which the powerful person will seem to offer to him; and he will lose the services which he will perform for the powerful or the general public of the city, or for magnates, and for the most part they will be reckoned as nothing. If it were the Lord of the 11th, he will not have friends who love him, unless on account of their usefulness, even if they pretend to be his friends; for indeed they will promise him much, but will serve him little or not at all. If however it were the Lord of the 12th, he will be practically unable to settle things regarding them;[189] and if he were to give them something in trust they will deny it, and will take something away from it, nor restore it, even if they were religious figures (unless perhaps they were forced to).

THE 121ST CONSIDERATION is that you look to see, in nativities or questions, whether the Moon is in the 8th, and the Lord of the Ascendant in the Ascendant, or in the 2nd, or in the 12th, retrograde: because this signifies that the native or querent will not have good fortune in games of dice, nor will dice "speak" good to him.

THE 122ND CONSIDERATION is that you look to see, in nativities or questions, whether the Part of Fortune is in the first 10° of the 4th house with the Head of the Dragon, the Moon, Venus and Jupiter, and they were direct: because it signifies that the native or querent will acquire immense wealth underground.[190] If indeed it were in the second 10°, with two of them, he will acquire it, but not in such a quantity; perhaps he will acquire a half, or near half [as much as he would in the first situation]. But if it were in the last 10° of the said house, and and it were with only one of them, he will acquire less again; however he will acquire it in a good quantity, perhaps one-fourth or perhaps near one-fourth. Which if the Part of Fortune were there alone, and it were free from the aspects of the malefics, he will acquire less again: for he will perhaps acquire one-sixteenth or less. If for example it were not one of these [situations], he will not acquire it, nor anything from it.

---

[189] *Non poterit quasi considere de aliquibus.* Unclear meaning.
[190] One wonders whether this Consideration is due to the higher volume of buried antiquities in Italy, or the frequency with which querents/natives asked about finding buried treasure. Perhaps in other areas one might merely make good on real estate.

Which if the Sun were then to aspect that place by a trine or sextile aspect [in one of the above situations], and the aspect were nearer to the first 10° than one of the aforesaid significators, it will be a treasure of raw gold; if however the Moon were closer, it will be silver. Which if Jupiter were closer, they will be diverse treasures, namely gold and silver and the like. If for example Venus were nearer, they will be pearls, womens' ornaments for the most part. If Mercury were nearer, they will be coins with sculpted images. But if they were retrograde, it signifies that the money will be offered [or shown] to him, but he will not acquire it for himself. But if one were retrograde and another direct, he will acquire part of it according to how many of them were direct.

Which if the Lord of the 8th house were then to aspect the Lord of the Ascendant from a square aspect or from the opposition, the discoverer will die because of it. If for instance it were to aspect by a trine or a sextile, it signifies that he will become gravely ill, but will not die from it. Which if it were the Tail instead of the Head, he will find it, but it will be taken away from him; or, led by ignorance, not knowing what it is, he will give it away for practically nothing. If indeed the Moon were then separated from the Lord of the Ascendant, and joined to a malefic who will impede her, he to whom the money is first given (by him who found it), will not pursue perceptible [physical], useful [ends] from it, or it will make much profit for him.[191] And if in addition Mars or the Lord of the 8th house were to aspect the Lord of the Ascendant then, the discoverer will be killed by those who take it away from him. Which if it were Mars and Saturn instead of Jupiter and Venus, the treasure will be ore, or copper, or lead, or other things of little value. If for instance the Lord of the Ascendant were with them then, or were to aspect them by any aspect, he who will find the treasure will become weary[192] from it (whatever kind of treasure it is, whether dear or precious, or of low quality).

THE 123RD CONSIDERATION is that you look to see, in nativities or questions, whether the Sun and Moon are joined in one and the same minute according to longitude and according to latitude, and one of the benefics is in the Ascendant, namely by 15' either below or above the line of the cusp, or 44' or less [and] below the line of the cusp: because it signifies that the native or querent will be fortunate in acquiring much substance, and in its accumulation, because a benefic will then be in the Ascendant. If indeed they were joined together in the

---

[191] *Non sequitur inde utilitatem quasi sensibilem, vel quod multum sibi proficiat.* I believe Bonatti is saying that it will be invested somehow, instead of being spent on physical possessions.
[192] Reading *fatiscet* for *fatescet* (1550) and *fatuescet* (1491).

the same minute according to longitude but not according to latitude, and their distance, namely of one from the other, were by 15' or less, his fortune will be in acquiring substance, but it will be less than this, in accordance as their distance were greater than 1' and less than 15'. But if the benefic who is in the Ascendant were below the line of the cusp by more than 15', up to 55', the fortune of the native of querent will be less than this, in accordance (as was said) as it were less than 15' up to 1', by proportioning from 15 up to 55, just as [the luminaries] are proportioned from 1 up to 15. You may say the same if the Moon were in the minute of the Sun's opposition, and a benefic were in the 7th, just as was said about the Ascendant: because a benefic will then be in the 7th, namely in the line of the cusp of the 7th house, which signifies the fortune of the native or querent because of wives or other women, and because of partners and enemies. But if, at the hour of the nativity, the Moon were in Taurus, in the minute of the Ascendant, so that Taurus is the Ascendant; or the Ascendant were Leo, and the Sun were in the minute of the Ascendant; nor did one of the malefics impede him or her, it signifies that the native will acquire much money, and he will reach great dignity and great exaltation. But if it were one of the malefics instead of the benefics (namely in the Ascendant or the 7th), it signifies the loss and destruction of the native's or querent's substance, by reason of the aforesaid.

THE 124TH CONSIDERATION is that you look, in nativities or questions, at the significator of the native's or querent's substance, and at the significator of his dignity or mastery, which you can understand from the Lord of the 10th house of the figure of the native or the question itself, or even from the Lord of the Ascendant, if the Lord of the 10th were not fit to signify the dignity or mastery of the native or querent–insofar as the quality of his nature and of his lineage were fit to assume dignity or mastery.

Which if the Lord of the 10th house (or its *al-mubtazz*) were oriental from the luminary whose authority it was,[193] and were elongated from it by 60° or more up to 90° (if it were of the superiors), or were elongated from it by 30° (if it were of the inferiors), and were in the angle of the 10th house or the Ascendant, so that it is not removed from the line of the angle (if it were beyond it) more than 30'. If indeed it were within it more than 1° 30', or were with the luminary whose authority it was, namely with the Moon and with the others, indeed with the Sun in his heart, and with the Part of Fortune, nor is it impeded, it will

---

[193] The Sun in diurnal figures and the Moon in nocturnal ones. But the description here pertains to the Sun.

signify that the native will rise to the dignity or mastery of his predecessors, and will not exceed that; but he will be greater and more excellent and more perfect in that dignity or in that mastery, then any one of his predecessors was. If however one of the aforesaid helping and fortunate fixed stars were in one of the aforesaid angles, with the Part of Fortune or with one of the planets, he will rise to a much greater dignity than any one of his relations had risen. Which if [the star] were of those which are in the first magnitude, and they[194] were the sole significatrices, the native or querent will rise to immense dignity, and immense honor, and to practically inestimable riches. If the Lord of the Ascendant were to aspect it, his fame and honor will reside in his own person; if however it were the Lord of the 2nd house [aspecting it], it will reside in his riches; if indeed [it were] the Lord of the 10th [aspecting it] he will reside in such a title and reign, as is fit for great kings, even if they were of low-class persons and a humble nation; and however much lower was their lineage, by that much more will he rise to a greater height. However, these will not last long; nor will they easily go beyond a space of 27 years,[195] and few will come to that, or to more than 30 years.[196] And by how much his degree[197] is higher, by that much more will his fall be heavier, and his dignity or title will be ended in evil, for it will come down to the ultimate misery: for indeed he will die a contemptible[198] or unseemly death. Which if this did not happen to him, it will happen to his more proximate successor in the dignity.[199]

THE 125TH CONSIDERATION is that you look to see, in nativities or questions, what sign is ascending: if it were the sign of a planet having two domiciles, the native or querent will be engaged in those things which are signified by the other domicile[200] of that planet, and its accidents will happen to him easily, and he himself will be the reason why they will happen to him.

---

[194] What does "they" denote, since he has named many candidates?

[195] This is the value in years given by Valens to Capricorn in certain profection procedures, a little less than Saturn's usual 30 lesser planetary years.

[196] Saturn's lesser years.

[197] *Gradus.* Bonatti must mean his social/political rank.

[198] *Vituperabilis*, lit. "blameworthy."

[199] This must be because of the fixed star, since Bonatti says later they make one rise and fall suddenly.

[200] Or "house," since it is by house position (whether using whole-sign or quadrant houses) that a sign comes to have a topical meaning.

For if it were Aries ascending,[201] he will be engaged in such things that he himself will be the cause of his own violent death or ruin,[202] because Scorpio (which is the other domicile of Mars) will then be the 8th domicile. Which if Mars were then well-disposed, and the Part of Fortune were in the 8th, he will be fortunate in whose things which are signified by the 8th domicile.

If it were Taurus ascending, he will be engaged in such things that he himself will be the cause of his own illness, because Libra (which is the other domicile of Venus) will then be the 6th domicile, whence he will be responsible for falling ill. Which if Venus were then well-disposed, and the Part of Fortune were in the 6th, he will be fortunate in those things which are signified by the 6th domicile.

If it were Gemini ascending, he will be engaged in such things they he himself will be the reason for his own capture, because Virgo ([which] is the other domicile of Mercury) will then be the 4th domicile. Which if Mercury were then well-disposed and the Part of Fortune were in the 4th, he will be fortunate in those things which are signified by the 4th domicile.

If it were Virgo ascending, he will be engaged in the things which pertain to dignity and exaltation, for he will acquire a realm by his own person and industry, and easily, without great labor or fatigue: because Gemini (which is the other domicile of Mercury) will then be the 10th domicile. If however Mercury were then joined with the Part of Fortune, and were in the Ascendant, he will acquire riches and dignities similar to a kingdom. Which if Mercury were in the 10th with the Part of the Kingdom,[203] and otherwise well disposed, namely fortunate and strong, without a doubt he will acquire a rulership or dignity which will be equivalent to a great king. Indeed, if in addition the Part of Fortune were in the 10th, and likewise the Moon, he will unmistakably become a great king.

---

[201] In this section I will speak of signs ascending instead of saying, e.g., "If Aries were the Ascendant," since Bonatti is clearly interested in the sign and not the degree of the Ascendant itself. Moreover, I will read *domus* as "domicile" (suggesting whole-sign houses), but Bonatti *could* mean quadrant houses and is simply *assuming* the ideal condition of not having any intercepted signs.

[202] Reading *occasi* for *occasio*.

[203] *Pars Regni*. This probably refers to the second Part of the 10th House in Tr. 8, Part 2, Ch. 13.

If it were Libra ascending, he will be engaged in the things which pertain to his ruin, and he himself will be the reason or occasion for his ruin, because Taurus (which is the other domicile of Venus) will then by the 8th domicile. Which if Venus were then well disposed, or the Part of Fortune were in the 8th, it signifies that he will be fortunate in those things which are signified by the 8th domicile.

If it were Scorpio ascending, he will be engaged in such things that he himself will be the cause of his own sickness, because Aries (which is the other domicile of Mars) will then be the 6th domicile. If for instance Mars were then well disposed, or the Part of Fortune were in the 6th, it signifies that he will be fortunate in those things which are signified by the 6th domicile.

If it were Sagittarius ascending, he will be engaged in such things that he himself will be the reason for his capture, because Pisces (which is the other domicile of Jupiter) will then be the 4th house. If for instance Jupiter were then well disposed, or the Part of Fortune were in the 4th, he will be fortunate in those things which are signified by the 4th house.

If it were Capricorn ascending, it signifies that he will be engaged in the things which will pertain to his profits, because Aquarius (which is the other domicile of Saturn) will then be the 2nd domicile. Which if Saturn were then well disposed, or the Part of Fortune were in the 2nd, he will be fortunate in those things which are signified by the 2nd domicile. If however he were poorly disposed, he himself will be the reason for the destruction of his substance.

If it were Aquarius ascending, it signifies that he will be engaged in things [such that] he himself will be the reason why he will acquire many hidden enemies for himself, because Capricorn (which is the other domicile of Saturn) will then be the 12th domicile. Which if Saturn were then well disposed, or the Part of Fortune were in the 12th, it signifies that he will be fortunate in the things which are signified by the 12th domicile.

Indeed if it were Pisces ascending, it signifies that he himself will be the cause of his own reign and his own title, *etc.*, as was said above when Virgo was the one ascending.

THE 126TH CONSIDERATION is that you look to see, in nativities or questions, whether Mercury is the significator of the nativity, or its participator,[204] and he is well disposed (namely fortunate and strong), and is in Capricorn or in Aquarius: because it signifies that the native will be of a profound and subtle character,[205] and of a high and great intellect, for he will understand in his heart [or deeply] the roots of things, of whatever type they were; and he will see from that principle to what end they can come to, and all the more strongly if then Saturn were to aspect Mercury (according to the quality of the aspect, nor were [Saturn] impeded); however [it will be] more so if Mercury were in Aquarius, in which is the joy of Saturn; and again more, if a benefic were then complected[206] with Mercury, or he himself [i.e., Mercury] were with one of the fortunate fixed stars. Which if he were in Aries or Scorpio, it signifies that he will be strong through stupidity and perfidy, and the agility of his motion, and magnanimity; and he will be arrogant around many people in his acts of arms; and he will be prudent, and quick to understand those things which are said to him, or he will understand what is written more than what is thought up by himself or through himself.[207]

THE 127TH CONSIDERATION is that you look to see, in nativities, if the Lord of the Ascendant of the nativity is naturally a malefic (as are Saturn and Mars), and ruled the nativity by himself without the participation of some benefic: because it signifies that the taste of the native, or his [sense of] smell, or his complexion, will not be similar to the taste or [sense of] smell or the complexion of others. For if Saturn were the sole significator, his taste will delight in tasteless, bitter [or briny], and sour things, as 'Ali[208] testifies in [his] exposition of the 40th statement in the *Centiloquy* of Ptolemy. If however Mars were the sole significator, he will delight in sharp and bitter things; he will not abhor agitated nor *circumnatum*[209] nor *pendulum*[210] wine, nor will he delight in what is sweet or

---

[204] See Tr. 9.
[205] *Ingenii. Ingenium* can also mean native talent or thinking.
[206] *Complexa*, lit. "embraced." In Tr. 3, Part 1, Bonatti speaks of the planets' "complexions" when they are in aspect, so this phrase means "in aspect to."
[207] These latter characteristics seem to describe a military man who is practical and ready to act, as opposed to forming his own strategies or thinking diplomatically.
[208] Probably 'Ali ibn Ridwān.
[209] Literally this means "around birth," which probably indicates freshly bottled wine.

delicate or clear; he will not abhor vile meats, nor even semi-rotten ones, nor even rotten or stinking fish; he will be inclined more to horrible odors than to sweet ones: like [those of] aloes, galbanum, serapine,[211] opoponax, the extinguishing of candles, the burning of leather, dung (both of stables and of other places), and the like. His nature will even delight in disreputable women, [and] ugly ones more so than beautiful ones; and will be more comfortable with them than with others. You may say the same about women, that they will delight more in ugly men than in handsome ones.

THE 128TH CONSIDERATION is that you look to see in nativities whether the Ascendant is formed in the image of the sign of a human, or its Lord is in a human sign, for if it were so, it signifies that the native will be housed[212] among men and will be readily joined with them. Which if it were a human sign ascending, and the Lord of the Ascendant were in a human sign, he will be more social[213] again, and associating himself with men, and conversing with them more freely. But if the Ascendant were a sign formed into the likeness of one of the animals which men use in their labors or in their actions (as are Aries, Taurus, and the last part of Sagittarius, [and] Capricorn) it signifies that the native will be humble with men, but he will not be very sociable with them. But if it were in the semi-feral signs (as are Cancer and Pisces), he will be again less sociable with them. If indeed it were in the feral and raging and woodland signs, as are Leo and Scorpio, he himself will be raging, and feral, and uncivilized[214] to men, nor would he want to be associated with one of them; for he would not want to be with parents or others of his blood-relatives.

THE 129TH CONSIDERATION[215] is that you look to see, in nativities, whether the Moon is exactly in the opposition of the Sun with one of the stars that are

---

[210] This could either mean "hanging" or "doubtful," so perhaps it indicates old or poorly bottled wine.

[211] *Serapinum*, a resin with an unpleasant odor related to asafetida.

[212] *Domesticus*, lit. "domesticated, private, belonging to a household."

[213] *Domesticus*.

[214] *Sylvestris*.

[215] This paragraph is a reworked and somewhat confused version of a passage in *Tet.* III.13. Ptolemy's list of conditions for showing damage to the eyes are as follows: (a) the Moon in the Ascendant or Descendant either at a New or Full Moon; (b) having a whole-sign aspect to the Sun and applying to a cloudy cluster of fixed stars; (c) Mars or Saturn, oriental of the Sun and occidental of the Moon (in the sign following hers), and angular; (d) Mars or Saturn, oriental of the Sun and occidental of the Moon, in the same sign as or in the opposite sign to, *both* luminaries (this affects both eyes).

called nebulous, which are *Al-thurayya*[216] and the Head of the Twins, and the Throat of Leo (which are said to be not very far from its heart), and others which, on account of their mixture with one another do not shine, when she is not distant from them by more than 10' according to longitude and according to latitude: it inevitably seems that the native is going to have illnesses in his eyes which cannot be cured by human medical means. Which if the Moon were then waning[217] in an angle, and Mars and Saturn were occidental from her,[218] not far removed from her, and [they were] oriental from the Sun, or they were opposite to each other and the Sun [were] in one of the angles, it signifies that the native will be deprived of the light of one of his eyes before the day of his natural death; nor does it seem he will be able to prevent it but that it will happen. Which if what was said were not so of both luminaries, but of only one of them, he will be deprived of the light of only one eye. If it were the Sun and he were a man, he will be deprived of the light of the right one; if it were a woman, she will be deprived of the light of the left one. But if it were the Moon and it were a man, he will be deprived of the light of the left one; if it were a woman, she will be deprived of the light of the right one.

THE 130TH CONSIDERATION is that you look to see, in nativities, whether the Moon is joined with Mercury by conjunction or by aspect, or one of the planets transfers light between them; which if it were not so, nor were the Ascendant a sign which is of the nature of Mercury or the Moon, and in addition Saturn were in an angle in diurnal nativities (and Mars in nocturnal ones), the native will be crazy[219] or raging or an epileptic or mentally deficient,[220] or foolish, or at least very forgetful—unless a strong benefic were then to aspect the Ascendant or Mercury or the Moon—and all the more powerfully if the angle in which one of the aforesaid malefics were, were Cancer (which is the exaltation of Jupiter) or Virgo (which is the exaltation of Mercury) or Pisces (which is the exaltation of Venus). And this is because the Moon in nativities signifies the body of the native, and the planet to whom she is joined signifies the virtues appearing in it, according to her own[221] virtue. If however she were joined to him or was going

---

[216] Lat. *Athozaic* (in Plato of Tivoli, *athoriae*), the Pleiades. Bonatti is misreading his account from a Latin edition of *Tet.* III.13. The list should read, "the nebula of Cancer *and* the Pleiades of Taurus."

[217] Lat. *occidentalis*, "occidental." Here I defer to Ptolemy.

[218] I.e., setting after her (Schmidt believes this should be in the sign following hers).

[219] *Amens*, lit. "without a mind."

[220] *Demens.*

[221] *Secundum virtutem suam.* It is possible this should be *suum*, referring to the virtues of the planet to whom she is joined. Bonatti is drawing from *Tet.* III.15.

to him [Mercury], he [the native] will be wise, and will preserve his sense, nor will he lose it. Which if Mercury were in Capricorn or Aquarius, not impeded, and he were of good condition, the native will be of great intellect and deep [or broad] understanding, wise, and a philosopher. Which if Jupiter and Venus were in the *kasmīmī* of the Sun, he will be a hermit, and practically a prophetic man, and his words will be heard and received before the other words of men.

THE 131ST CONSIDERATION[222] is that you look to see, in nativities, if it were the nativity of a man, whether the Sun and the Moon are both in masculine signs, or are both in one masculine quarter, or in one masculine signs: because if it were so, this signifies that the actions of the native and his workings will be natural in insofar as they pertain to men, and he will engage in them naturally. But if it were the nativity of a woman, and the luminaries were so disposed (as was said), she will be mannish,[223] and will engage naturally in the things which pertain to men, and she will despise men. And if she were to marry, she will not want to revere her husband, nor be subject to him. Which if Venus and Mars were in masculine signs in the nativity of a man, he will have the ordained sexual intercourse according to nature and law. If indeed they were oriental, he will abound in sexual intercourse, and will be excessive in the manner of it, and will not be content in natural sexual intercourse, but rather will have a yearning for lewd sex and will despise women and be used by men. If however they were occidental and were in feminine signs, his sexual intercourse will be unnatural and unclean; and all the more so if Saturn (who signifies unclean sexual intercourse) were to aspect them. If indeed it were a woman, and Mars and Venus were in masculine signs, and were oriental, she will abhor sexual intercourse with men, nor will she delight in it; she will rather delight in the rubbing of women, and especially girls. But if Mars and Venus were in feminine signs and were occidental, she will love sexual intercourse with men, and will delight in it, and will be used by a man according to nature. And if Jupiter were in a feminine sign and were occidental in nativities of both men and women, nor

---

[222] Coley abbreviates this Consideration, which is a rearranged and somewhat confused version of a passage in *Tet.* III.15. There are too many differences to enumerate, so I will simply say that for Ptolemy, (a) both luminaries in signs of one gender will make the native excessive in pursuing the typical sexuality of that gender (i.e., in masculine signs, both men and women will be excessive in pursuing women or in acting masculine); (b) Venus and Mars both made masculine or feminine along with the luminaries (i.e., both in masculine quarters while both luminaries are in masculine signs, or in feminine quarters while both luminaries are in feminine signs) will make the already-excessive native do shameful and debased things; (c) but if only Venus or only Mars is made similar to both of these luminaries, Venus will make the behavior secret, while Mars makes it public.

[223] *Virago.*

were it the case for Mars as was said about him, the sexual intercourse of the native will be natural and according to law. If for instance Mars were the sole significator, nor did Jupiter aspect him, their sexual intercourse will often be against the laws, both natural and apostolic. And Ptolemy said in his *Centiloquy*,[224] [if] Venus will be incorporated[225] by Saturn, and he [or she?] had dignities in the 7th, he will be born of unclean sexual intercourse.

THE 132ND CONSIDERATION is that you look to see, in nativities, whether Mars (in nativities) is corporally with a certain red star of his nature, which is in Taurus, which is called Algol, so that there is a distance of 16' or less between them, with Mars going toward it, and the Lord of the domicile (or the exaltation or two of the other dignities) in which is the luminary that is the authority (which is called the Lord [of the] *An-nawbah*)[226] is in the opposition of Mars or in his square aspect, nor does one of the benefics aspect the ascending degree, nor is it[227] in the 8th house [domicile?]: it is far from doubtful [that it] signifies that the native will be decapitated.[228] Which if the latitude from Mars to [the star] were not more than 16', it will happen infallibly, nor will he be able to escape it unless God averts it. Which if a retrograde or combust benefic were to aspect the rising degree, the native will nevertheless hardly be able to prevent it but that the native will be decapitated, but he will not be decapitated because of his own fault. If however it were not retrograde, it will release the native from an evil death: he will go away by his own choice, but he will die by a fatal disease which will appear from a hot cause, and this before his fiftieth year. Which if it were not so concerning Mars as was described, and a malefic were in the 8th, the native will die an evil death. If however there were a benefic there [in the 8th], not impeded, he will die in his own home by a common death. If for instance the benefic were impeded, he will then die from something unpleasant overtaking him.

And[229] Ptolemy said in his *Centiloquy*[230] that if there were a luminary in the Midheaven whose authority it was, I say with the aforesaid conditions, the

---

[224] Aph. 80.

[225] *Incorporabitur.* That is, in corporal conjunction with.

[226] Lat. *Anauba*, from Ar. النوبة, "the deputyship," with the connotation of a periodic return to perform a duty—as the luminaries alternate in assuming the sect rulership once each day. This doctrine is based on *Tet.* IV.9; for *an-nawbah*, see *JN*, p. 11. I am still uncertain whether *an-nawbah* really refers to the luminary sect ruler, or (as Abu 'Ali implies) to the triplicity rulers of the luminary sect ruler.

[227] Who?

[228] See also Aph. 83.

[229] This passage is Bonatti's own, not Lilly's (as Coley's edition makes it seem).

native will be hanged. Which if one of the malefics were then in Gemini and the other in Pisces, his hands or feet will be cut off according to what is signified (I say) by the sign in which you find the one who was more malicious. If for instance Mars were corporally joined with the Lord of the Ascendant, and they were in Leo, nor did Mars have any dignity in the Ascendant, nor were one of the benefics in the 8th [domicile][231] it signifies that the native will be burned. Which if Mars were then retrograde or combust or cadent, this will happen to him of his own fault. If however it were not impeded, it will happen to him for reasons he did not deserve. And Ptolemy said[232] that if Saturn were in the nativity, I say, in the Midheaven, and he whose deputyship[233] it was, were opposite him, and the fourth sign [were] dry, the native will die by means of [falling] ruins. If indeed it were moist, he will be drowned. Which if it were in the form of a man, he will be strangled. Again, if one of the malefics (namely Mars or Saturn) were in the Ascendant at the hour of the nativity, and were peregrine, the native will have a mark or sign on his face or head. Which if it were impeded, retrograde or combust, the mark or sign will be notable or nasty. If however it were free [from impediment], it will not be nasty.

THE 133RD CONSIDERATION is that you look to see, in nativities, whether the Ascendant is Gemini or Sagittarius, and the Lord of the Ascendant were well disposed, namely fortunate and strong, and likewise the Moon. Because it signifies that if the native were to survive, he will acquire much substance. Which if the Ascendant were Virgo or Pisces, and the Lord of the Ascendant and the Moon were well disposed, he will acquire money and spend it in a good way; and he will live largely and splendidly; and he will be loved by men on account of his largesse and the goodness of his life. He however whose Ascendant were Gemini or Sagittarius, will not be a good spender, but stingy. Yet he whose Ascendant were Gemini or Virgo, could lose his substance, and be reduced to poverty by it. Indeed he whose Ascendant were Sagittarius or Pisces, will never lose it nor will he be reduced to poverty itself. Moreover, look to see if the Ascendant were Aries or Scorpio or Capricorn or Aquarius, because the native will be avaricious and miserable, and shunned. But if Jupiter were then to aspect the Ascendant, it will reduce the misery, however it will not remove it.

---

[230] Perhaps Bonatti is thinking of *Tet.* IV.9; but there it is Mars who is supposed to be in the Midheaven.
[231] This must indicate whole-sign houses, following Ptolemy.
[232] Aph. 76.
[233] Lat. *Anauba*. See note above.

THE 134TH CONSIDERATION is that you look to see, in nativities, whether Mars and Venus are in the 6th and otherwise well disposed: because it signifies that the native is naturally going to be an accomplished doctor in some area of medicine. And[234] if Mercury were joined corporally to Venus, and she retrograde, it signifies that the native will naturally be an accomplished singer. But if Mercury were in the 12th, nor otherwise impeded, it signifies that he will naturally be wise in all sciences and philosophies.

THE 135TH CONSIDERATION is that you look to see, in nativities, whether the Lord of the Ascendant and the Moon, and Jupiter and Venus, are all in the Ascendant, or Jupiter and Venus aspect the Lord of the Ascendant and the Moon in the Ascendant by a trine or sextile aspect, nor are they impeded: because if it were so, it signifies that the native is going to be very strong in body, and that none will dare to neglect his commands.

THE 136TH CONSIDERATION is that you look to see, in nativities of kings and wealthy and great men (namely of those those who are fit to rule), if both luminaries were in the degrees of their exaltation, or in their domiciles in such a degree, one in the kind the other was,[235] and they were free from all impediments: because it signifies that the native will attain to great and sublime dignities: for he will become the king of the Romans, or someone close to that who is in a royal dignity below the king of the Romans, so that it will be said of them that he is practically a universal king in the world, and this will be extended up to the fourth generation of his descendants. But if every planet who is below Jupiter were to commit its disposition to him, and he were receive it from every one of them (not ignoring the aforesaid condition), and after he were to commit them and his own[236] to Saturn, and Saturn were to receive them and him, and they were both oriental from the Sun and in angles, it signifies that the native is going to be a great man of a great and powerful name, even if not a royal one; it will attach his name in the earth, and his fame will last for a long time for his whole life, and after his death it will last for three reigns of Saturn,[237] or perhaps more.

THE 137TH CONSIDERATION is that you look to see whether Mercury is joined with Saturn in the Ascendant: because it signifies that the native will be

---

[234] Presumably this point is unrelated to the point about Venus and Mars in the 6th.

[235] *Unum in quali fuerit alterum.* I believe this simply means that they cannot be in different types of dignity, i.e., one in the degree of its own exaltation and the other in its own domicile.

[236] Reading *suam* for *suas.*

[237] I.e., 90 years. In the 141st Consideration below, Bonatti describes one reign as being the 30 year period of the Saturn return (also Saturn's lesser years).

foolish, talkative, and wishes to be reputed wise; he will speak bad about everyone, both men and women. The greater wisdom which will be found in him will be to invent great lies and to use them; he will hardly be able to talk but that he will mix something of falsity with his speech; indeed it will be natural for him to lie, and he will have a very filthy tongue, and he will also have a malicious tongue from Saturn, [and] indeed from Mercury his sharpness of malice.

THE 138TH CONSIDERATION is that you look to see, in nativities, whether in someone's nativity there are two malefics in the bound of the 4th house of that nativity, or if the angles were movable signs and Mars and Saturn were in them: because it signifies that the native will be poor, miserable, and unfortunate beyond all other unfortunate people for the whole time of his life, unless Jupiter (or the Lords of the triplicity of the Ascendant) works against it.

THE 139TH CONSIDERATION is that you look to see, in nativities and likewise in questions, in which house [domicile?] the Tail of the Dragon is found: because it signifies the voiding and destruction of things which are signified by that house, and particularly wealth.

For if it were in the first, it signifies the voiding of wealth which the native made with his own person. If it were in the second, the voiding of wealth which he will have made with his own money or substance. If it were in the third, the voiding of wealth which he will have made with his brothers or on account of his brothers, or with neighbors or lesser blood-relations. If it were in the fourth, the voiding of wealth which he will have made with his father or uncle or father-in-law, or an inheritance, and it even signifies that the native or querent will change many houses because of improvements, nor will he remain firmly in them, nor will it go well for him in his moving. If it were in the fifth, the voiding of wealth which he will make with his children or on account of children. If it were in the sixth, the voiding of wealth which he will make with slaves or smaller animals. If it were in the seventh, the voiding of wealth which he will make with women or partners or enemies.[238] If it were in the ninth,[239] the voiding of wealth which he will make with religious figures or because of religious figures. If it were in the tenth, the voiding of wealth which he will make because of dignities or masteries. If it were in the eleventh, the voiding of wealth which he will make with friends or because of friends. But if it were in

---

[238] The eighth is missing in both 1491 and 1550.
[239] The 1491 edition substitutes numbers for the rest of the houses, but I will continue to put them in the masculine/neuter form.

the twelfth, the voiding of wealth which he will make with larger animals or because of hidden enemies.

THE 140TH CONSIDERATION is that you look to see whether the significator of the end of the matter or of its fulfillment is so weak that it cannot perfect the matter–likewise the Moon. If it were so, then take the significator of the querent and the significator of the quaesited matter, and subtract the lesser from the greater; and add the degrees of the ascending sign to the remainder, and project what comes out of that from the Ascendant; and where it were to fall, the Lord of that sign will be his significator which you seek according to the content[240] of the quaesited matter or considered topic, and you will judge according to its condition, as you were to find him fortunate and strong, or unfortunate and weak. For if it were done concerning substance, and it were in the second, the substance of the querent will be disposed according to its condition. If it were in the third, the brothers will be disposed according to it; if it were in the fourth,[241] the older blood-relatives will be disposed according to it; if it were in the fifth, the children will be disposed according to it; if it were in the sixth, the slaves [or domestics] will be disposed according to it; if it were in the seventh, the wives wil be disposed according to it; if it were in the eighth, the dowries will be disposed according to it; if it were in the ninth, long journeys will be disposed according to it; if it were in the tenth, his masteries will be disposed according to it; if it were in the eleventh, his friends will be disposed according to it; if it were in the twelfth, his enemies will be disposed according to it.

THE 141ST CONSIDERATION is that you look in nativities and consider the gifts or fortunes which are given to men by the fixed stars, and the manner of their durability in their subjects,[242] and why they do not last so long in them as long as those things which are given by the planets, when they seem to ought to last for a longer time than them–about which [matters] I remember finding nothing else said, except that Ptolemy said in his *Centiloquy*[243] that the fixed stars give gifts beyond measure, but oftentimes they end in evil. And al-Mansur said in his chapters[244] (offered to the great king of the Saracens), the fixed stars give

---

[240] *Substantiam.*

[241] The text now substitutes Arabic numerals, but I will continue to use the masculine/neuter form.

[242] *In suis subiectis.* Bonatti means the bodies and events which they influence, that which is "subject" to their influence.

[243] Aph. 29.

[244] *Capitulis.* This refers to the *Chapters of al-Mansur*, Proposition 27.

grand gifts, and lift up from poverty to loftiness, which the seven planets do not do.

The gifts which the fixed stars give to men, do not last in them as long as those which the planets give. It happens therefore that the fixed stars are agents [or act] and men are patients [or undergo]. Whence the subjects in which stars act, are not appropriate for them, nor are they born fit to be able to receive their impression. For it is necessary that between an agent and a patient there be some conformity or some appropriateness. Indeed the fixed stars have the slowest motion, and the slowest changes, and therefore their impressions require subjects or patients suited for them, and which are of the longest durability, and which have conformity with them so their effect can be perfected or completed in them. For the circular motion of the fixed stars is not completed in less than 36,000 years. Indeed the circular motion of men lasts for three reigns of Saturn[245] (which is the slowest of the planets), which is a space of 90 years. Few pass beyond that, which can happen to some people by the addition of the years of some planet to the years of the al-kadukhadāh[246] in the root of the nativity. Whence often, or rather mostly, the length of life of a man is 90 years, even if some octogenarians or perhaps nonogenarians lie and say they are centogenerians when in truth they are not; which has neither true conformity, nor any similarity, with the 36,000 years to perfect the effects of their [the stars'] impressions.

For just as an eagle cannot extend nor exercise the full amount of his flight, nor his power, into a fly's, nor can a stone going out from the sling of a catapult exercise its actions on a bed of moss, so the fixed stars cannot exercise the full amount or effect of their impressions in men; and therefore their gifts or fortunes do not last in men a long time, because men have much faster changes, and are of little durability in comparison with the circularity of the fixed stars.

And therefore it was said, "use the fixed stars in the building of cities; indeed the planets in the building of homes,"[247] because among corruptible things cities are things of very long durability in comparison with houses; indeed a house is of long durability in comparison with men. For indeed houses do not always last

---

[245] I.e., three Saturn returns.

[246] Lat. alcocoden or alcochoden, Ar. الكدخذاه (see al-Qabīsī, IV.5). According to Kunitzsch (1977, pp. 35-36), it is a Persian version of the Greek oikodespotēs, or "master of the household." But the al-kadukhadāh in medieval astrology is strictly limited to questions of longevity, whereas an oikodespotēs in Hellenistic astrology has a broader meaning of rulership.

[247] Source unknown.

in an undivided way.[248] Indeed cities last through the successive building and rebuilding of houses. However castles, even though they are of long durability, are not of as much [durability] as cities are. Whence we can use the superior planets in building castles, however it is more prudent to use fixed stars in their building, because castles are of greater durability than homes, even if sometimes certain castles are taken apart. And because cities are of greater durability than castles, they are still nearer to the fixed stars, whose subjects they are; for the impression which a solid thing makes in a more solid thing, lasts longer than in a less solid thing. Again, it lasts much less in a thing that is not solid than in something that is a little solid; and again it lasts much less in a soft[249] thing than in something not solid or less soft.

Whence the impressions which the fixed stars make in cities are of greater durability than those which they make in castles, because cities are more correlated to them in terms of their long length of time. And those which they make in castles are of greater durability that those which they make in houses, because castles are closer to their correlation than houses are. Indeed the bodies of men are more removed from [the stars'] bodies than houses are, and therefore are more corruptible; and therefore their significations apply less to them; and if they are applied to them, they last less, because the things signified by the fixed stars are both great and noble, and high; and far from corruption and changeability, so that they cannot quickly sustain a changeable commixture with quickly corruptible or fast-changing things, unless like oil and water do; for even if it imprints in it, still the impression does not last long.

For the fixed stars perform with such nobility that on account of their most remote elongation from corruptible, and vile, and fast-changing things, and their approach to the supernal splendor, their significations cannot remain long in them, or with them, and especially in men, since they are changed and corrupted easily and quickly–or rather, most quickly; and especially in those low in birth and feeble and faint of heart: for they do not go beyond the person of him whom they touch, and when he is living it rarely happens otherwise (and most of the time to his evil), and in such a way that God alone could avert it (and not another, as I often say). Because *sometimes* they can be ended in good, even if it

---

[248] *Per ipsarum individua*, lit. "through their undivided things." When put in connection with the next sentence, Bonatti seems to mean that while cities endure during the changes in their houses, houses endure during the changes to their parts. But Bonatti has put it in an odd way, and I suspect the printed text might contain an error. See Tr. 7, Part 2, 4th House, Ch. 3.
[249] *In re lubrica*. This word, which really has connotations of slipperiness, is not really an opposite to "solid," but the point is made.

rarely happens, just as it sometimes happens that some people will have lived according to the greatest years of the *al-kadukhadāh*,[250] concerning whom in my time I have not seen, except for one man who was called Richard, who said he had been in the court of Charlemagne,[251] King of France, and had lived 400 years. And it used to be said then that there had been a certain other man who was from the time of Jesus Christ, and he was called John Buttadaeus[252] because he had struck the Lord when He was being led to the gibbet; and He said to him, "You will wait for me until I have come." And I saw [the aforesaid] Richard in Ravenna in the era of Christ 1223, and this Joannes crossed through Forlì, going to St. Jacob's in the era of Christ 1267.

Nor would the significations of the fixed stars have applied to men, nor could they stick to them, nor last in them practically perceptibly, unless there were a medium through which they act in them (the planets, which are the secondary agent, and the fixed stars the principal one); for wherever there are many actions set in order, attributed to diverse agents, it is necessary that the principal [original] action be allotted to the principal agent, because they comport themselves toward the effecting of corruptible things as much as the first cause. Indeed the planets are just as much the second cause. For the corruption which these inferior things undergo, is on account of their exceeding remoteness or distance from the incorruptible superiors, which are not said to have motion, since they do not seem to be moved sensibly. However they endure sometimes in magnates and the wealthy, who are fit for a kingdom and are magnanimous and great of heart, of whom one in my own time was Frederick II, Emperor of Rome—who, when he was needy and placed in a

---

[250] Here Bonatti is clearly allowing that some people could live to practically antediluvian ages.

[251] *Caroli magni*, i.e., Carolus Magnus, or Charles the Great. Charlemagne was King of the Franks from 771 AD–814 AD.

[252] John Buttadaeus is a medieval name for Cartaphilus, a legendary porter for Pontius Pilate, who struck Jesus at some point before the Crucifixion. The medieval legend conflates him with one of the Apostles, using Jesus's statement in John 21:22, saying "If it is my will that he remain until I come, what is that to you?" John is also known as the Wandering Jew, because he was supposed to have traveled Europe for centuries, waiting for Christ's return. Clearly Bonatti believes (or at least reports others' testimony) that John passed through his own hometown in 1267. One version of the legend says that John falls into a trance every century, and awakes as a young man—thus making it possible for any young charlatan to pass himself off as John! See the review of George K. Anderson's *The Legend of the Wandering Jew* by Utley (1968), who says this legendary John is probably meant to be Malchus, the slave whose ear was cut off in the Garden of Gethsemane.

position of great necessity,[253] he was made Emperor with no one able to resist him, and to him [went] Apulia, the Kingdom of Sicily and Jerusalem, Krakow,[254] Italy, the Roman Empire except for the area of[255] Lombardy. And he even subjugated his treacherous enemies and the rebels, and he remained fast in such a position for nearly 30 years. Ultimately however he died miserably, he was poisoned by his own men, and his whole family was destroyed, so that practically none of them remained in one piece.[256]

There was a certain other man, Ezzelino da Romano, who, though he was not very lofty, was exalted high above all Italians, so that his fame crossed over the seas and sounded through many regions. For he was lord over practically all of the Mark of Treviso, even up to Germany[257] and up to Trent,[258] and up to near Venice by four or five *miliaria*; and he remained tyrant in those parts, and his tyranny lasted for 26 years. Ultimately however all of these things were ended in his evil.[259] For when it seemed impossible that he could be oppressed, he fell into the hands of his greater enemies whom he had [beaten] in a certain battle which he had carried in the companionship of the men of Milan[260] at Cassianum,[261] and he died miserably, and all of his family was destroyed, with none remaining.[262]

Likewise there was a certain man of the realm of Apulia, of low stock, named Piero della Vigna, who, when he was a scholar in Bologna used to beg, nor did he have anything to eat. And afterwards he was made a clerk, then chief clerk of the court of Emperor Frederick II. After that he heard laws and was made the greater judge of the court of the Emperor, and rose to such dignity that he who could get a little bit of the fringe [of his cloak] was reputed to be blessed by his

---

[253] Although Frederick was the son of an Emperor and raised (at least in word) by a Pope, he lived in low circumstances until he entered into an arranged marriage with Constance, daughter of the King of Aragon.

[254] Lat. *Cracovia.*

[255] *Prater partem*, which could also mean "except for a part of."

[256] *Penitus*, lit. "deeply, completely."

[257] Lat. *Alamania.*

[258] Lat. *Tridentum* (mod. Ital. Trento).

[259] *In eius malum*, lit. "into his evil." Bonatti's biographical sketch does not explain whether his death (a) exposed, proved, or was the culmination of his evil; or (b) was evil in the conventional sense that violent deaths are an evil, generally speaking. Indeed, virtually all of the men Bonatti now describes were arrogant and ruthless men who also died violent deaths. At any rate, this phrase does not really affect Bonatti's main point, which is that being set in a high station by the fixed stars is likely to lead to being plummeted down again.

[260] Lat. *Mediolanensis.*

[261] *Quod gessit in comitatu Mediolanensi apud Cassianum.* The *comitatus* was the feudal institution of the *comites* (sing. *comes*), household warriors originally housed by a lord, and fighting for him.

[262] See a biographical sketch of Ezzelino in the Introduction.

grace; and whatever he did, the Emperor used to approve. He, however, many times retracted and infringed upon what the Emperor did. And the Emperor made him lord or ruler of all of Apulia, and in goods he was found to have in gold alone 10,000 Augustan *livres*, apart from other riches which were said to be practically inestimable. In the end, since indeed he came to such a low state [or depression] and to such misery, that the Emperor had him blinded, he, moved by [the Emperor's] disdain, smashed his head against a certain wall, and thus killed himself miserably, just as then common opinion said.[263]

There was even a certain other man from Pisa who was called Smergulus, of low stock, practically from the lowest of people, who was practically made lord of the Pisans; nor were any of the magnates bold enough to resist him; afterwards he was brought down to nothing.

After him there was a certain other man in the same city who was called Oddo Gualduzius, from a small [clan of] people, who rose to such a height, that he practically dominated the whole city, nor was there anyone bold [enough] to contradict him; ultimately a certain man who was a judge, [named] Galiver, caused him to be cut into pieces[264] in the city of the Pisans; nor did the authorities make any rule from then on except that he who behaved evilly, suffered harm.[265]

The same happened in Forlì with a certain man who was called Simon Mestaguerra, who was born of a low father, who came to such high status, that the whole populace followed him; nor did anyone dare to resist him, except for me alone (who had known him as he really was); and whatever evil he could do, he did against everyone, and this lasted practically three years. Ultimately however he was put down, and came virtually to nothing, for he was banned and expelled from the city, which happened on account of the vileness of his body and his faint-heartedness.[266]

Likewise[267] there was a certain brother of the Order of Preachers[268] named John, Vicenzan by birth, whom I have named elsewhere,[269] who was considered

---

[263] Piero della Vigna's suicide was rumored; but he was certainly fired and imprisoned on charges of embezzlement (and other offenses) by Frederick II in 1249, and died that same year. See van Cleve (1972), pp. 520-23.

[264] Reading *frustatim* for *frustratim*.

[265] *Nec aliquod regimen fecit inde potestas, nisi quod qui habuerit malum, passus est damnum.*

[266] Perhaps this means that people realized he was a cowardly, wretched man; but Bonatti phrases it oddly. Simon Mestaguerra was expelled in 1257.

[267] The fact that Bonatti spends so much time on John is probably due to (a) the time he spent in trying to verify his miracles; and because (b) Bonatti was active in Bologna, where John exercised his influence.

[268] I.e., the Benedictines.

holy by practically all the Italians who confessed the Roman Church; but to me it seems that he was a fake:[270] he came to such a high status, that he was said to have raised eighteen dead people, of which none could be seen by anyone; and he was said to cure every illness, to cast out demons—I however could not see anyone freed [from illness], even though I put forth much effort to see [them]; nor [did I see] anyone who firmly said that he had seen one of his miracles, and it seemed that practically the whole world was hastening after him, and he who was able to have a thread from his cape was considered blessed, and [the thread] was kept like holy relics. And the Bolognese used to go armed with him, and around him in a group,[271] and they used to surround him with arched staffs wherever he went, lest someone be able to approach him; and if some people did approach him, they would deal with them harshly. For some used to kill,[272] others wound, others fall on them powerfully with clubs; and he himself rejoiced and was happy about the hacked-up victims[273] and the wounded, nor did he heal any of them as Jesus did Malchus.[274] And he used to say openly in his speeches that he spoke with Jesus Christ, and likewise with the Blessed Virgin, and with the angels whenever he wanted to. And the brother Preachers in Bologna then, under such nonsense, earned (according to what was said publicly) more than 20,000 silver Marks; and his power was so great in Bologna that the Bolognese feared him to the degree that whatever he preached to them they did—in fact at one time he caused to be released a certain soldier named Laurencerius, who had killed the son of one of his neighbors and had been condemned to be decapitated by the authorities; nor were the authorities bold [enough] to do anything against his rule, nor was anyone bold enough to contradict his orders, except for me alone—but not the Bolognese; for I knew his tricks and his lies; but the vulgar man was saying that I was a heretic solely out

---

[269] This must be the same John mentioned in Tr. 1, Ch. 13, described as a condemner of astrology. In 1233 he was a leader of the popular "Alleluia" peace movement, and was later the Duke of Verona. Based on the lengthy description here, and the personal enmity shown by him to Bonatti himself, Bonatti must have taken great delight in his downfall.

[270] *Hypocrita*, a mime who follows another's performance, or a hypocrite. Here Bonatti does not mean hypocrisy in our sense, but a fake or poseur.

[271] *Pro communi.*

[272] *Mactabant.* I am tentatively assuming Bonatti means "kill" and not "punish," since the phrases decrease in severity and "wound" is similar to "punish."

[273] *Mactatis caesis,* lit. "the hacked-up people who were killed." Since it is somewhat unclear whether Bonatti is using *macto* to mean "kill" or "punish," I have tried to phrase it broadly here.

[274] Remember, John was reputed to be a great healer.

of fear of him, and he remained in that state[275] for nearly one year; ultimately however he was brought down to nothing, so that he was hardly associated with by a single Brother when he wanted to go somewhere, and men started to understand who he was.

THE 142ND CONSIDERATION is that you look, in nativities or universal questions, at the gifts or fortunes which are given to men by the planets, because they are applied to them, and last a long time with them, and are extended to their successors in accordance with how they are disposed in the roots of nativities; but not excessively, unless perhaps they will be applied to by the fortunate fixed stars; and for this reason because they are of quick changeability, whence they have more affinity with them than do those things which are given by the fixed stars, and especially the fortunes which are given by the inferiors, on account of their greater velocity and their conformity with the subjects correlated to them. Indeed the fortunes which the superiors give, do not last as long in humans as the aforesaid; however they have value [or are strong] in the building of houses more than others.

On the fortunes which Saturn and the other planets give[276]

For Saturn, when he is oriental [and] well disposed (namely fortunate and strong and received in the place in which he is) gives great fortunes in buildings, the planting of trees, the long durability of those looking into the cultivating of lands, in the management of waters,[277] and the like.

Indeed Jupiter gives great fortunes in the sciences, like laws, making decisions, decrees, and in dignities, like judgeships, bishoprics, and the like.

However Mars gives great fortunes in the raising of armies, and leading them,[278] and the like.

Indeed the Sun gives great fortunes in lay dignities like kingdoms, the ruling of cities, positions of civil authority, and the like.

---

[275] I.e., condition or status.
[276] Coley (pp. 68-69) wrongly attributes this passage to Lilly, who at any rate does not translate the whole passage.
[277] *In productionibus aquarum.*
[278] *Ducatibus.*

Indeed the inferiors give their own great fortunes adhering to men, and things more durable than the superiors do in corruptible things (which are inferior to cities and castles), on account of [the inferiors'] nearness to [corruptible things], and the speedy and quick change to those receiving them, and their correlation with them. Indeed Venus, who is the superior planet of the inferiors, gives her fortunes in those things which pertain to the doings of women and their ornaments (and in seducing them so they do not protect themselves from men), and wealth because of them, and the like.

However Mercury gives his fortunes from mercantile activities, writings, paintings, future things, and the like.

Indeed the Moon gives her fortunes from navigation and mercantile activites which are often recounted even in writings and paintings; the planting of vines; engaging in drinking or the selling of wine and its trade, and the like.

All these are given excellently if [men] adhere to those things which are naturally given by the planets, as I said. And even though the significations of the bodies of the supercelestials adhere in men, still they do not always last in them; however the significations of the inferior planets last a longer time than the significations of the superiors; and the significations of the superiors last longer than the significations of the fixed stars.

For example, the significations or fortunes or riches which are given by the Moon can last up to the seventh age or generation, because she is the seventh planet after Saturn, when beginning from the superiors; and if they were to go beyond the seventh, they cannot go beyond the eighth (by putting an age or generation from the 42nd year up to the 45th, so that both are included). Those which are given by Mercury can last up to the sixth age, because he is the sixth planet after Saturn; indeed they cannot go beyond the seventh, and hardly attain it. However, those which are given by Venus can last up to the fifth age, because she is the fifth planet after Saturn. Indeed they cannot go past the sixth, and they hardly attain that. Indeed those which are given by the Sun can last up to the fourth age, because he is the fourth planet after Saturn; they cannot go beyond the fifth and hardly attain that. Indeed those which are given by Mars can last up to the third age, because he is the third planet after Saturn; they cannot go past the fourth, and hardly attain that. Those which are given by Jupiter can last up to the second age, because he is the second planet after Saturn; indeed they cannot go beyond the third, and hardly attain that. Indeed those which are given by Saturn can last up to the one age; at all events they cannot go beyond, and hardly or never attain, the second.

And even though I said that they can last that long, still I do not say that they will not be finished before that; for Aristotle said[279] that there are posited limits which cannot be crossed; but he did not say that they cannot be reached,[280] and so it is with this. For indeed I say they cannot go beyond the aforesaid [ages] without either being destroyed wholly or being pressed down such that they will remain in such a condition that it will not be likened to the thing before, unless as something green or blackish [is] to the very white, unless perhaps something happens anew from another source (which rarely happens). Nor could it be truly said that it truly would be the same, but rather it was something else from the start.[281]

And of the aforesaid there were certain people who wanted to say that such riches or the like could be said to be bad to seek, and thence it was treated such that the laity [would be] near destruction from [such] profit from bad sources. For they said that profit from bad sources do not go beyond the fifth age; and certain ones said that they do not go beyond the third, not knowing however whence they had it, unless they were to hear it being said by others for a long time (and because they saw it often come out that way). Nor however is it without some reason by the aforesaid conditions, namely that profit from bad sources does not go beyond the third or fifth age. For by profit from bad sources I understand riches which come to someone in the manner of interest and of things in which many lies are committed, and many deceptions, and pillage and theft, and the like.[282]

---

[279] Bonatti may be drawing on Aristotle, *Met.* Δ.17 (a discussion of limits) rather than his discussion of infinitude in *Phys.* III. The "limits" involved seem to be the ages at which the natural life of the body will be ended–this is not a primarily numerical limit, but a limit to the body's endurance which we *measure* numerically.

[280] Reading *perveniri* for *praeveniri*.

[281] Unusual passage and confusing comparisons: *quod non assimilabitur priori, nisi ut viride vel subnigrum albissimo, nisi forte aliquid accidat noviter aliunde, quod rarius continget; nec poterit vere dici quod sit illud idem, immo erat aliud a primo.*

[282] The general meaning of this paragraph is clear, though the individual sentences are odd and seem to lack a verb here and there. The meaning is: profit from things like interest or activities involving deception will not last or be inherited through generations.

THE 143RD CONSIDERATION is that you consider the manner of judging, and by what routes you must reach some judgment, so you can examine it and rightly analyze it,[283] and according to how the stars show you their truth to be disclosed. The method of whose consideration is this, for you will look at this in fourteen ways:

The first way is whether the querent asks from an intention or not. For if the Lord of the Ascendant and the Lord of the hour were the same, or the signs in which the aforesaid significators were, were of the same triplicity or the same complexion, the question will come to be from an intention. If indeed it were not so, or the Ascendant were the end of some sign, the question will not be from an intention, nor rooted.

Second, look at the Ascendant and its Lord, and the Moon, and the planet from which she is being separated, and give them to the querent. Indeed you will give the seventh and the planet to which the Moon is joined to the quaesited, as is said elsewhere. And if it were necessary, go down to [specific] people according to how things are signified by the houses, from the 1st up to the 12th.

Third, you will consider the house [domicile?] or sign signifying the quaesited matter.

Fourth, the aspect of the benefic or malefic planets to the significators of the quaesited matters.

Fifth, in which place from its own domicile any of the significators were, whether in its own, or in the 2nd or in the 3rd or in the 4th, and so on, up to the 12th;[284] or [if any] were in the *via combusta*, or it is found in similar places.

Sixth, whether it is found in the angles or succeedents or cadents.

Seventh, attend diligently to whence the querent's aid will come to him, namely whether from the father or the child or the king, or blood-

---

[283] *Discutere.*
[284] In this case Bonatti clearly means whole-sign houses.

relatives or friends, *etc.* Because the good [or benefic] significators will judge good, the bad ones [or malefics] the contrary.

Eighth, by the happiness of the querent (like if the Lord of the first is found in the fifth or joined anywhere with its Lord apart from the impediment of the malefics) or through his sorrow (if it is found in the 6th or the 7th or the 8th or 12th) unless the question is about matters which are signified by those houses; for you will judge according to what you were to find.

Ninth, by the benefics or malefics according to how you were to find them in places signifying things about which questions come to be, like if there were more benefics, good; if however if there were more malefics, evil; if equally good, you will announce a middling [result].

Tenth, if the Lord of the first were in the house of the quaesited matter, or found anywhere with its Lord.

Eleventh, that you consider in which house the Lord of the first were conjoined with the significator of the quaesited matter: because you could judge the matter that is going to come, by the significator of that house or its fit time.[285]

Twelfth, if the significators were not conjoined and one of the planets were to transfer light between them, or were to accept their disposition, you will judge the same.

Thirteenth, by the nature of the significators toward each other, in the natures and significations in which they agree.[286]

Fourteenth, you will pronounce according to whether the receiver of disposition were benefic or malefic, strong or weak, and were to aspect the significators or the Moon (or one of them) from friendship or enmity.

---

[285] *Occasione.* This word can mean "opportunity" (which doesn't seem right) or "fit time" or "proper moment." Bonatti may be referring to the timing of events as measured by its applications to other planets.
[286] Or perhaps, "in the significations of what they agree in" (*concordantium significationibus*).

THE 144TH CONSIDERATION is that you consider, in questions or in nativities or other beginnings, when the significators do not well show you what you intend to know, and their signification is ambiguous, nor could you well weigh it. Take the place of the Lord of the Ascendant, and the place of the Lord of the domicile of the Moon, and see the distance in degrees which is between them (beginning from Aries[287]), from which you will make signs.[288] And add from above the degrees of the ascending sign, and project from the Ascendant both in the day and at night, and where the number were ended, the Lord of that house [domicile?] will be the significator, and you will take from him the signification of the quaesited matter; for you could judge according to his disposition.

THE 145TH CONSIDERATION is that you look to see, in diurnal nativities, if *Cor Leonis* were in the Ascendant, namely in the eastern line, or above it by 1° or less, or below it by 3°; or [if] it were in the 10th, in similar degrees without the conjunction or aspect of a benefic; because this will signify that the native will have a great name, and great power, [and] likewise be exceedingly exalted, and that he will reach to sublime dignities, even if the native were found to be of the lowest-class parents. And if again one of the benefics were to aspect the place, his sublimity will be augmented more. If however the nativity were nocturnal, it will be somewhat less than this, but not much. Which if the malefics were to aspect, it will be somewhat more below that. If indeed the benefics were to aspect, they will increase its goodness by one-fourth, and will decrease the malice by one-fourth. But, nevertheless, whichever of the aforesaid it was, it signifies that the native will die a bad death, or at least all of his sublimities and all his greatnesses and his powers will be ended in evil.

THE 146TH CONSIDERATION is that you look at the place of the Lord of the Ascendant, and the place of the Lord of the twelfth, and subtract the lesser from the greater, and add the degrees of the ascending sign to the remainder, and project from the Ascendant; and where the number were ended, the Lord of that sign will be a participator with the Lord of the question; and he will be called the first participator. Again, look at the place of the Lord of the said sign,[289] and the place of the Lord of the Part of Fortune, and subtract the lesser from the greater, and add the degrees of the ascending sign, and where the number were finished, the Lord of that sign will be a participator, and he will be

---

[287] I.e., in the order of signs.
[288] I.e., convert the distance into 30° increments for easier reckoning.
[289] I.e., look at the place where the first participator is actually located.

called the second participator. Which if they were one and the same planet, you will look only at him. You will even look at the said participators (namely the first and the second), and subtract the lesser from the greater, and add the degrees of the ascending sign, and the planet in whose domicile the number were to fall, will be the third participator; and whichever of the three is stronger, will be said to be more authoritative in the participation of the quaesited matter.

Which if the remainders[290] (or two of them), were to fall in the domicile of one planet, he is to be preferred. Which if the question seems to be good,[291] and the participators are badly disposed, they subtract from the good which is signified by the question. But if they were well disposed, they will increase the good. If however the question were found to be bad, and the participators are found to be well disposed, they will decrease the evil which is signified by the question. If however they were badly disposed, they will increase it.

There are even many other considerations which could be ascribed to and considered with the aforesaid, but it would be most involved for you, and very and severely complicated. You however from your own industry could give attention to them in their own place and time, if they occur to you. I will make mention of certain ones of them in the Treatise on judgments, certain others in the Treatise on elections, certain others in the Treatise on revolutions, even certain ones in the Treatise on nativities, certain others in the Treatise on rains or changes of the air, just as you, if you were to attend diligently to them, could investigate them if it pleased you.

---

[290] Not the remainders, but the place where the final sums fall.
[291] By "question," Bonatti means "the judgment of the chart of the question."

BIBLIOGRAPHY

Abu Bakr, *Liber Genethliacus* (Nuremberg: Johannes Petreius, 1540)

Abū Ma'shar al-Balhi, *The Abbreviation of the Introduction to Astrology*, ed. and trans. Charles Burnett, K. Yamamoto, and Michio Yano (Leiden: E.J. Brill, 1994)

Abū Ma'shar al-Balhi, *Liber Introductorii Maioris ad Scientiam Iudiciorum Astrorum*, vols. VI, V, VI, IX, ed. Richard Lemay (Naples: Istituto Universitario Orientale, 1995)

Abū Ma'shar al-Balhi, *The Abbreviation of the Introduction to Astrology*, ed. and trans. Charles Burnett, annotated by Charles Burnett, G. Tobyn, G. Cornelius and V. Wells (ARHAT Publications, 1997)

Abū Ma'shar al-Balhi, *On Historical Astrology: The Book of Religions and Dynasties (On the Great Conjunctions)*, vols. I-II, eds. and trans. Keiji Yamamoto and Charles Burnett (Leiden: Brill, 2000)

Abū Ma'shar al-Balhi, *The Flowers of Abū Ma'shar*, trans. Benjamin Dykes (2nd ed., 2007)

Al-Biruni, Muhammad ibn Ahmad, *The Chronology of Ancient Nations*, trans. and ed. C. Edward Sachau (London: William H. Allen and Co., 1879)

Al-Biruni, Muhammad ibn Ahmad, *The Book of Instruction in the Elements of the Art of Astrology*, trans. R. Ramsay Wright (London: Luzac & Co., 1934)

Al-Fārābī, *De Ortu Scientiarum* (appearing as *"Alfarabi Über den Ursprung der Wissenschaften (De Ortu Scientiarum)*," ed. Clemens Baeumker, *Beiträge zur Geschichte der Philosophie des Mittelalters*, v. 19/3, 1916.

Al-Khayyat, Abu 'Ali, *The Judgments of Nativities*, trans. James H. Holden (Tempe, AZ: American Federation of Astrologers, Inc., 1988)

Al-Kindī, *The Forty Chapters (Iudicia Astrorum): The Two Latin Versions*, ed. Charles Burnett (London: The Warburg Institute, 1993)

Al-Mansur (attributed), *Capitula Almansoris*, ed. Plato of Tivoli (1136) (Basel: Johannes Hervagius, 1533)

Al-Qabīsī, *Isagoge*, trans. John of Spain, with commentary by John of Saxony (Paris: Simon Colinaeus, 1521)

Al-Qabīsī, *The Introduction to Astrology*, eds. Charles Burnett, Keiji Yamamoto, Michio Yano (London and Turin: The Warburg Institute, 2004)

Al-Rijāl, 'Ali, *In Iudiciis Astrorum* (Venice: Erhard Ratdolt, 1485)

Al-Rijāl, 'Ali, *Libri de Iudiciis Astrorum* (Basel: Henrichus Petrus, 1551)

Al-Tabarī, 'Umar, *De Nativitatibus* (Basel: Johannes Hervagius, 1533)

Al-Tabarī, 'Umar [Omar of Tiberias], *Three Books of Nativities*, ed. Robert Schmidt, trans. Robert Hand (Berkeley Springs, WV: The Golden Hind Press, 1997)

Alighieri, Dante, *Inferno*, trans. John Ciardi (New York, NY: Mentor, 1982)

Allen, Richard Hinckley, *Star Names: Their Lore and Meaning* (New York: Dover Publications Inc., 1963)

Aristotle, *The Complete Works of Aristotle* vols. I-II, ed. Jonathan Barnes (Princeton, NJ: Princeton University Press, 1984)

Bloch, Marc, *Feudal Society*, vols. I-II, trans. L.A. Manyon (Chicago: University of Chicago Press, 1961)

Bonatti, Guido, *Decem Tractatus Astronomiae* (Erhard Ratdolt: Venice, 1491)

Bonatti, Guido, *De Astronomia Tractatus X* (Basel, 1550)

Bonatti, Guido, *Liber Astronomiae: Books One, Two, and Three with Index*, trans. Robert Zoller and Robert Hand (Salisbury, Australia: Spica Publications, 1988)

Bonatti, Guido, *Liber Astronomiae Part IV: On Horary, First Part*, ed. Robert Schmidt, trans. Robert Hand (Berkeley Springs, WV: The Golden Hind Press, 1996)

Boncompagni, Baldassarre, *Della Vita e Della Opere di Guido Bonatti, Astrologo et Astronomo del Seculo Decimoterzo* (Rome: 1851)

Brady, Bernadette, *Brady's Book of Fixed Stars* (Boston: Weiser Books, 1998)

Burnett, Charles, ed., *Magic and Divination in the Middle Ages* (Aldershot, Great Britain: Ashgate Publishing Ltd., 1996)

Burnett, Charles and Gerrit Bos, *Scientific Weather Forecasting in the Middle Ages* (London and New York: Kegan Paul International, 2000)

Carmody, Francis, *Arabic Astronomical and Astrological Sciences in Latin Translation: A Critical Bibliography* (Berkeley and Los Angeles: University of California Press, 1956)

Carmody, Francis, *The Astronomical works of Thābit b. Qurra* (Berkeley and Los Angeles: University of California Press, 1960)

Dorotheus of Sidon, *Carmen Astrologicum*, trans. David Pingree (Abingdon, MD: The Astrology Center of America, 2005)

Grant, Edward, *Planets, Stars, and Orbs: The Medieval Cosmos, 1200–1687* (New York, NY: Cambridge University Press, 1994)

Haskins, Charles H., "Michael Scot and Frederick II," *Isis*, v. 4/2 (1921), pp. 250-75.

Haskins, Charles H., "Science at the Court of the Emperor Frederick II," *The American Historical Review*, v. 27/4 (1922), pp. 669-94.

Hermes Trismegistus, *Liber Hermetis*, ed. Robert Hand, trans. Robert Zoller (Salisbury, Australia: Spica Publications, 1998)

Holden, James H., *A History of Horoscopic Astrology* (Tempe, AZ: American Federation of Astrologers, Inc., 1996)

Ibn Labban, Kusyar, *Introduction to Astrology*, ed. and trans. Michio Yano (Tokyo: Institute for the Study of Languages and Cultures of Asia and Africa, 1997)

Ibn Sina (Avicenna), *The Canon of Medicine (al-Qanun fi'l tibb)*, ed. Laleh Bakhtiar (Great Books of the Islamic World, Inc., 1999)

Kennedy, Edward S., "The Sasanian Astronomical Handbook Zīj-I Shāh and the Astrological Doctrine of 'Transit' (Mamarr)," *Journal of the American Oriental Society*, v. 78/4 (1958), pp. 246-62.

Kunitzsch, Paul, "Mittelalterliche astronomisch-astrologische Glossare mit arabischen Fachausdrücken," *Bayerische Akademie der Wissenschaften Philoso-phisch-Historische Klasse*, 1977, v. 5

Kunitsch, Paul, trans. and ed., "Liber de Stellis Beibeniis," in *Hermetis Tris-megisti: Astrologica et Divinatoria* (Turnhout: Brepols Publishers, 2001).

Kunitzsch, Paul and Tim Smart, *A Dictionary of Modern Star Names* (Cambridge, MA: New Track Media, 2006)

Latham, R.E., *Revised Medieval Latin Word-List from British and Irish Sources* (Oxford: Oxford University Press, 2004)

Lemay, Richard, *Abu Ma'shar and Latin Aristotelianism in the Twelfth Century* (Beirut: American University of Beirut, 1962)

Levy, Raphael, "A Note on the Latin Translators of Ibn Ezra," *Isis*, v. 37 nos. 3/4 (1947), pp. 153-55.

Lilly, William, *The Starry Messenger* (London: Company of Stationers and H. Blunden, 1652). Reprinted 2004 by Renaissance Astrology Facsimile Edi-tions.

Lilly, William, *Anima Astrologiae*, trans. Henry Coley (London: B. Harris, 1676)

Lilly, William, *Christian Astrology*, vols. I-II, ed. David R. Roell (Abingdon, MD: Astrology Center of America, 2004)

Long, A.A. and D.N. Sedley, *The Hellenistic Philosophers*, vol. I (Cambridge: Cambridge University Press, 1987)

Māshā'allāh *et al.*, *Liber Novem Iudicum in Iudiciis Astrorum* [Book of the Nine Judges], ed. Peter Liechtenstein (Venice: 1509)

Māshā'allāh, *De Receptione* [*On Reception*] and *De Revolutione Annorum Mundi* and *De Interpraetationibus*, in *Messahalae Antiquissimi ac Laudatissimi Inter Arabes Astrologi, Libri Tres*, ed. Joachim Heller (Nuremberg: Joannes Montanus and Ulrich Neuber, 1549)

Māshā'allāh, *On Reception*, ed. and trans. Robert Hand (ARHAT Publications, 1998)

Maternus, Firmicus Julius, *Matheseos Libri VIII*, eds. W. Kroll and F. Skutsch (Stuttgard: Teubner, 1968)

Michelsen, Neil F., *The Koch Book of Tables* (San Diego: ACS Publications, Inc., 1985)

Mantello, F.A.C. and A.G. Rigg, eds., *Medieval Latin: An Introduction and Bibliographical Guide* (Washington, DC: The Catholic University of America Press, 1996)

New Oxford Annotated Bible, ed. Bruce M. Metzger and Roland E. Murphy (New York: Oxford University Press, 1994)

Pingree, David, "Astronomy and Astrology in India and Iran," *Isis* v. 54/2 (1963), pp. 229-46.

Pingree, David, "Classical and Byzantine Astrology in Sassanian Persia," *Dumbarton Oaks Papers*, v. 43 (1989), pp. 227-239.

Pingree, David, *From Astral Omens to Astrology: From Babylon to Bīkāner* (Rome: Istituto italiano per L'Africa e L'Oriente, 1997)

Pseudo-Ptolemy, *Centiloquium*, ed. Georgius Trapezuntius, in Bonatti (1550)

Ptolemy, Claudius, *Tetrabiblos* vols. 1, 2, 4, trans. Robert Schmidt, ed. Robert Hand (Berkeley Springs, WV: The Golden Hind Press, 1994-98)

Ptolemy, Claudius, *Tetrabiblos*, trans. F.E. Robbins (Cambridge and London: Harvard University Press, 1940)

Ptolemy, Claudius, *Quadripartitum* [Tetrabiblos], trans. Plato of Tivoli (1138) (Basel: Johannes Hervagius, 1533)

Sahl ibn Bishr, *Introductorium* and *Praecipua Iudicia* [The Fifty Judgments] *De Interrogationibus* and *De Electionibus*, in *Tetrabiblos*, ed. Girolamo Salio (Venice: Bonetus Locatellus, 1493)

Sahl ibn Bishr, *De Electionibus* (Venice: Peter of Liechtenstein, 1509)

Selby, Talbot R., "Filippo Villani and his Vita of Guido Bonatti," *Renaissance News*, v. 11/4 (1958), pp. 243-48.

Seneca, *The Stoic Philosophy of Seneca*, ed. and trans. Moses Hadas (New York: The Norton Library, 1968)

Stegemann, Viktor, *Dorotheos von Sidon und das Sogenannte* Introductorium *des Sahl ibn Bišr* (Prague: Orientalisches Institut in Prag, 1942)

Thomson, S. Harrison, "The Text of Grosseteste's *De Cometis*," *Isis* v. 19/1 (1933), pp. 19-25.

Thorndike, Lynn, *A History of Magic and Experimental Science* (New York: The Macmillan Company, 1929)

Thorndike, Lynn, *The* Sphere *of Sacrobosco and Its Commentators* (Chicago: The University of Chicago Press, 1949)

Thorndike, Lynn, "A Third Translation by Salio," *Speculum*, v. 32/1 (1957), pp. 116-117.

Thorndike, Lynn, "John of Seville," *Speculum*, v. 34/1 (1959), pp. 20-38.

Utley, Francis Lee (review), "*The Legend of the Wandering Jew* by George K. Anderson," *Modern Philology*, v. 66/2 (1968), pp. 188-193.

Valens, Vettius, *The Anthology*, vols. I-VII, ed. Robert Hand, trans. Robert Schmidt (Berkeley Springs, WV: The Golden Hind Press, 1993-2001)

Van Cleve, Thomas Curtis, *The Emperor Frederick II of Hohenstaufen: Immutator Mundi* (London: Oxford University Press, 1972)

Weinstock, Stefan, "Lunar Mansions and Early Calendars," *The Journal of Hellenic Studies*, v. 69 (1949), pp. 48-69.

Zoller, Robert, *The Arabic Parts in Astrology: A Lost Key to Prediction* (Rochester, VT: Inner Traditions International, 1989)

Zoller, Robert, *Bonatti on War* (2nd ed., 2000)

INDEX